UNTHINKABLE CHOICE

THE SAMPSON PARKER STORY

by

SAMPSON AND LEE ANN PARKER

WITH THOMAS SMITH

[signature]

Comfort PUBLISHING

UNTHINKABLE CHOICE

For information, address Comfort Publishing, 296 Church St. N., Concord, NC 28025. The views expressed in this book are not necessarily those of the publisher.

First printing

Book cover design by Reed Karriker
Photo by Michael A. Anderson Photography

ISBN: 978-1-938388-43-9
Published by Comfort Publishing, LLC
www.comfortpublishing.com

Printed in the United States of America

DEDICATION

I dedicate this book to my wife Lee Ann for her never ending love and support, without her this book would have never been written and the message that God has led us to share would be lost. She has encouraged me and yet kept me grounded during this entire process. You are an amazing woman Lee Ann. Thank you for your countless hours and constant encouragement. I love you more than you will ever know.

For God so loved the world that he gave his one and only Son,
that whoever believes in him shall not perish but have eternal life.
John 3:16

"Teacher, which is the greatest commandment in the Law?" Jesus replied:
"Love the Lord your God with all your heart and with all your soul
and with all your mind. This is the first and greatest commandment.
And the second is like it: Love your neighbor as yourself."
Matthew 22:36-39

"On this day five years ago, my dad was faced with a life or death situation.
Most people would have probably given up; however, my dad fought through
several hours of intense pain while battling to save his life. He managed to
sever his own arm from a corn picker to free himself. He is without a doubt
the biggest hero and fighter that I know. It still amazes me how positive he
has been and how much of a leader he is and always was.

Dad, I love you and can't thank you enough for what you did
to still be with Mom and me today."

Sampson Parker, Jr.
September 11, 2012

II.

There is no doubt in my mind that Sampson is here today by the grace of God. The strength that Sampson mustered to do what he did, the fact that he did not give up, the fact that he didn't bleed to death, and all the interventions that allowed him to be set free from the corn picker and cared for by just the right people, was all thanks to God. The fact that he was able to come out of all of this without bitterness, hate, and remorse is just more proof of God's grace.

Many people have commented on my strength and positive attitude since Sampson's accident, and they ask how I was able to hold it altogether.

It wasn't something I did on my own.

Many times I wanted to curl up and cry. There were many times when I thought, I can't go through this. I'm not cut out to do this. And there were times I felt left out and alone. All the attention seemed to be flowing towards Sampson (and rightly so), but human nature kicked in and I begin to feel sorry for myself.

So how did I overcome all of this?

It was the power of prayer from God's people praying for us all around the world.

It was more than just knowing they were praying. I truly *felt* their prayers. It's hard to explain, but in many cases I felt a sense of peace when peace should have been the last thing I was feeling. There were times when I knew everything would work out even though I had no idea how things would work out. I felt down in the dumps and exhausted one minute and then I felt my attitude improve, and was rekindled and ready to continue caring for my husband. I went through times of doubt and pity and in the next breath I would feel a sense of encouragement and fulfillment because I would put the feelings and needs of others before mine.

It was all about prayer and answered prayers. Prayers for Sampson. Prayers for our family and friends, and prayers for me as I nursed him back to health.

This was my first experience on this side of prayer.

I have always been what some refer to as a prayer-warrior, but I have never been in a situation where I was on the receiving end of others praying for me. When I prayed for others, I really never knew how my prayers would be answered or what the others were experiencing. Now I do. I have learned from this experience that both sides of prayer are a true blessing from God and that I will never second guess the effects of praying for a total stranger.

I was a person practicing her faith before the accident, but I've seen a major change in my faith since the accident. I have felt the life-sustaining gifts from God first hand. The gifts I am speaking of are the gifts we receive when we accept Jesus Christ as our personal savior: The fruit of the Spirit, love, joy, peace, patience, kindness, goodness, faithfulness, gentleness, and self-control. (Galatians 5:22-23)

Before Sampson's accident I thought of these gifts like unique Christmas gifts. I am referring to the ones you get and you aren't too sure what to do with them. You receive them, are excited about getting them, thankful for having them, and even cherish them. But at the same time you're not too sure what to do with them so you store them away only to pull them out from time to time for special occasions. This is how I used the gifts of the Holy Spirit. I knew I had them. They were tucked away and ready to use, but I didn't use them often enough to really appreciate them. Then I would search for them when I needed them and put them to use the best way I knew how.

Today I carry those gifts with me everywhere I go, and I look for ways to use them. Using these gifts has sustained me and has helped me to help Sampson with his recovery. They have also helped us adapt to our new "normal" way of approaching life and its tasks.

Lee Ann Parker

FORWARD

I've heard it said all my life that God works in mysterious ways, and based on my experience, I have to agree.

The title of this book is *Unthinkable Choice* for a number of reasons. Before we go much further, don't get the idea that I think I'm a particularly super human person, because I'm not. If that were the case, then I would have come out of this whole ordeal without so much as a scratch like Superman when bullets bounce off his chest in the comic books and on the movie screen.

But that didn't happen with me.

I was wounded all right. Inside and out.

Over the years people have seen my story on TV or read about it in newspapers and magazines, and many of those people have made it a point to stop me and talk about it. Some even call me a hero. I may be many things, but a hero is not one of them. I'm a man who did something pretty stupid and, by the grace of God, lived to tell about it. The real heroes in all of this are the people who stopped to help me when I was bleeding beside the road, the doctors and nurses who were waiting when I came to the hospital, the EMTs and helicopter crew who moved me from place to place, and all the people who took me by the hand and guided me through the dark days after the accident.

They are the real heroes.

And while we're on the subject of heroes, my family certainly falls into that category.

But me? I'm just a man who made a near-fatal mistake and felt the power of God first hand.

And while I realize I am not invincible, I have always had this feeling of invincibility. I stand over six feet tall, have always been in good health, and I thrive on challenges and hard work. I grew up in and around the coal mines of Kentucky where simple, hard-working adults raised equally hard-working kids, who later grew up to be hard-working adults. It's just the way I was raised. Those were the cards I was dealt, so to speak.

I played basketball in high school and was good enough that I could have played in college. The thing is I didn't want to go to college. All I wanted to do was find a job where I could run a bulldozer and do a good day's work for a good day's pay. I was willing to get whatever training I needed to do the job, even if that meant going to a technical school, but basically, I wanted to bypass college and go straight to work.

So that's what I did.

I had the world by the tail. I was doing what I felt like I was created to do.

I felt invincible.

I also feel blessed and have felt that way my whole life. Blessed to have an appreciation for hard work. Blessed by every opportunity that has come my way. Blessed to have a family that I love and that loves me. Blessed to have good friends. I have always believed in God and always acknowledged the fact that He is the one who made it all possible. He is the one who has done all the blessing.

But for the longest time, that was the extent of my relationship with God. I believed in God and knew that he was the source of all the good things in my life. But when it came to sharing what I knew with others, I was usually busy with either work or family and didn't notice other people as much as I should have.

I was a Christian with a very small view of the world.

On that note, I was never baptized as a child, but it wasn't for lack of trying. I made a run at it many times, but was never able to follow through. I was raised Baptist and always wanted to do it. I knew I probably should do it. And every Sunday I would sit there through the service, perched right on the edge of my seat, almost ready to go.

Almost.

But then when the altar call came, I was scared to take that final step. Scared to take the actual walk down the aisle and make a public proclamation of the things I felt in my heart. I'd hear the words and feel them deep within me. But I just couldn't make myself actually leave the pew and walk down to the altar.

So for most of my life, I was comfortable with the relationship I had with God, though as I look back I'm not too sure God was as comfortable with it as I was. But He is patient. So He just waited until the time was right, and then stepped in as only He can. I guess God touches people in different ways, and maybe what happened to me is what it took for Him to touch me and get my attention.

And He sure got it.

When I talk about what happened and God's part in it, people sometimes ask me if I think He caused the accident.

No.

I was able to do that all by myself through my own carelessness…or stupidity. Some days, I'm not sure which it was. But no, I've never thought He caused it. I did it all by myself.

But what I *do* believe is that He used that situation to reach me and ultimately push me along my Christian journey. And through my unique circumstance, He has allowed me to help other people in ways I never could have imagined.

I'm a simple man with a simple view of life. I believe in a God who loves us so much that He sent His Son to die for us. I believe that family is the bedrock on which everything else in our lives is built, and without that bedrock, society suffers. I believe that the United States is the greatest country in the world, and even though we have our problems, we offer more hope to the world than any other place *in* the world. I believe our military men and women, whether they are fighting on the front lines or ordering supplies stateside, are deserving of our respect and admiration. And I believe that God can use any and every one of us to make a difference right where we are.

I don't pretend to understand how God works. But I do know that I've felt God at work through me and have seen God at work in the lives of many of the people I've been fortunate enough to meet. For example: I'm a shy guy, and for me to get up and tell my story in front of 450 women at a church conference, that is all God's doing. For me to tell my story to millions of people on the Today Show or some other TV program is not something I could do on my own. I take no credit for things like that.

God is leading me into things I would never have thought about doing before the accident.

Several people have told me that by seeing me on TV or reading about my story in an interview, and my bringing God into the picture, helped them. And that says more about God than it does about me, because I'm just a one-armed man living life the best way I know how. But as long as God is willing to take what I've been through and show other people something about how much He loves all of us, then I'm ready and willing to do my part. If I can touch just one person with my story, then it has been worth it.

And that leads me to one last thing.

The real invincible thing: love.

The Bible says "God is love." That makes sense to me.

I have experienced love in so many forms over the last few years that I can't begin to describe them all. I have experienced the love of God through the love of my family, the love of my friends, and through the love-filled moment when I was battling for my life and called out to God and He answered me.

So believe me when I say this: Love saved my life.

Sampson Parker

ACKNOWLEDGEMENTS

After my accident Lee Ann and I agreed that we would never forget to share with those we told our story to that if it weren't for the grace of God I would not be here today. So first and foremost we acknowledge and give thanks to God for giving me this second chance at life and for guiding us though out the process of bringing you our story. We would also like to acknowledge and give thanks to the following:

To those of you who came to hear my story and afterward shared with me that I needed to write a book I thank all of you. It was through your kind and caring words that I heard God's message and endured the ups and downs and disappointments in this process. Discerning God's timing was our biggest challenge.

To Doug Spinks, my first responder, for his knowledge, expertise, calmness and efforts to make sure I had every chance of surviving. Thank you my friend, we will always have a special bond.

To Karen Baker who calmed and cared for me while waiting on the ambulance, my sweet angel.

To our parents, siblings and children, friends, neighbors, church families, and co-workers, your daily encouragement and prayers were a Godsend. We couldn't have done it without your continuous inquiries on how the book was coming and the motivation it brought to the process. Your part in making this book a reality will never be forgotten.

To my son Sampson Jr., for stepping up to the plate and taking on responsibilities beyond his years and his sincere love and respect during the time of the accident and beyond.

To our other two children Tiffany Bub and Luke Watson for their calls and prayers during the time of the accident and to their spouses Burgess and Faith for all of their continued love and support.

To Helen and Keith Lukens for being there in every way imaginable for me, my wife, and my son, from the moment they got the call about my accident and up to this point and beyond.

To my brother Steve Parker, his wife Delia and son Colt who were by my side during the whole time of my recovery and for all they did and do to help my family.

To my mother, Helen Parker for her endless prayers and concern. Also her church, East Pineville Baptist Church of Pineville, KY for their abundant prayers and support for her during the first few months after my accident.

To my sisters Gale Smith and Joyce Garrity for their visits and prayers.

To my brother Ronnie and his wife Pam for their visit and prayers.

To my brothers Randy, and Roger for their calls, cards, prayers, and support.

To Lori Kay Kienzle, Lee Ann's sister, for being there for my wife and all her love and support along the way.

To Sheri, Lee Ann's sister, and Marty Few for their witness, prayers, and support.

To Chris, Melanie, Heather and Cody Johnson for being there to support Sampson Jr. and taking care of Decoy.

To our extended family in Florida, Thanks Matt and Carole Haley!

To all the Blythe Construction Employees. With a special thanks to Bill Capehart and Alan Cahill for their sincere concern for me and my family and assurance that my job would be there for me once I recovered.

To Judy Sellers (my temporary personal secretary), retired Blythe Human Resource Manager.

To Brian and Sally Webb who came to Augusta numerous times and who went out of their way to support me, my wife, and my son.

To Steve Burleson, Blythe's Equipment Manager and his assistant Jason Mauney who refurbished my company truck and made sure I was able to start it with ease.

To Mitch Galyon and Terry Hensley who helped to organize the Home Coming Cook Out and worked in the Corn Pick'In.

To all the Corn Pick'In "Pickers" who came to the farm with equipment and energy for a hard day's work: Steve Parker and family, Helen and Keith

Lukens, Sheri , Marty and Bobby Few, Dale and Sheila Hall, Charlie and Jeff Herndon, Lisa and Shawn Phipps, Terri, Tim, Josh, Justin and Kayla Carraway, Pete Rabon, Terry Hensley, Mitch Galyon, Jason Mooney, Wayne Wilson, Kyle Laney, Michael Croxton, Otis Dabbs, Mr. Peach, Laney Truesdale, Mr. Stover, Bill Childers, Terry Threatt and kids. They picked, and bagged over five hundred 80 pound bags of corn! A special thanks to Terri and Tim Carraway for documenting the event with pictures and video. Also a special thanks to Marty and Sheri Few for feeding the crew.

To all the participants and guests at the "Home Coming Cook Out" on the farm. A special thanks for the monetary donations given by the Blythe employees, friends, and family which was used to purchase cover crop seed. And to GML Inc. – Joe Turner, family and employees for the donation of his equipment, fuel and operators to disc and plow 20 acres in rye in preparation of next year's corn crop. A special thanks to the Blythe cooks – Wayne Ramsey, Mark Spradley and Tim Marsh who fed over 75 guests and the employees and friends who handpicked over 50 bags of corn.

To Cox Brother's Farm: Marion and Delano Cox and all the other family members for their love and support during my recovery and their encouragement to continue farming.

To Oliver Paving Inc., Charlotte, NC – Ken Oliver and family

To LPA Group, Charlotte, NC

To my wife's employer at the time, Gary D. Morgan, CPA, P.A. and staff, for being so understanding.

To our neighbors at Stallings Glen Subdivision in NC for food, cards, and prayers and support during my time of recovery and throughout the years after my accident.

To Rocky River Presbyterian Church, Harrisburg, NC for food, cards, and prayers with a special thanks to Alice Williams for the personal occupational therapy house calls.

To Liberty Hill Presbyterian Church, Liberty Hill, SC – Dr. Rollins' for his hospital visit in August, GA, and to our home in NC. Also a special thanks to all the LHPC members and friends for their prayers, and cards.

To each and every person, some known and many unknown, who sent cards (over 150) and those all around the world who prayed for my family and me.

To all the staff, nurses, physician assistants, and doctors at Palmetto Richland Memorial Hospital, and Doctors Hospital who cared for me with true kindness, concern, and professionalism. And the Christian ministry provided by many, many churches in Augusta, Georgia during our stay at Doctors Hospital.

To the physical and occupational therapists and doctors at Carolinas Medical Rehabilitation, especially Dr. Sharon Kanelos, for all their special care and for helping me adjust to life with one arm and a helper arm.

To the staff and prosthetist at Faith Prosthetics and Hanger Prosthetics for designing, building, and continually repairing, my prosthetic arm and their ongoing encouragement.

To the writers who worked with us along the way instilling ideas and giving us the direction that ultimately lead us to Thomas Smith, we thank you for the critical part you played in getting us there. It was through Thomas's belief that it was in God's plan to share this story and his Godly talents that our story was taken to the next level.

Lee Ann and I realize that even in this extensive list we may have inadvertently left off those who should have been listed. Please know that if we did so it was not done intentionally; so, for all others who have crossed our paths during this journey and are not listed we give you thanks.

And finally to Comfort Publishing, thank you for believing that our story was meant to be shared.

CHAPTER 1

Except for its historical significance, the day started out like every other workday. It was Tuesday, September 11, 2007, and I was driving to work. But that morning my mind wasn't on my job. I was thinking about my farm. That and the terrorist attack on our country six years earlier.

As a highway project superintendent for Blythe Construction Company, I work on large highway projects. There's a lot of planning and logistics work involved; dealing with people, watching over each project assigned to me, and seeing to it that the job is completed on time and under budget. Put all that together and it can be stressful, but I love my job.

But even with all the planning and meetings, it's not a desk job by any stretch of the imagination. Being a superintendent requires me to be outside onsite, and as someone who loves the outdoors and enjoys the challenge of working outdoors, it is a perfect fit for me. It brings me a lot of physical and mental satisfaction.

But emotionally — that's a different matter.

Emotionally, my heart is drawn to a fifty-acre farm in Camden, South Carolina, just north of Granny's Quarter Creek. It's a place I've worked to make it into what it is today. A place that represents everything I hold dear in life. It's a retreat. A family place. A sanctuary.

It's the place I go to get away.

Whereas my day job can be stressful, the farm is just the opposite. It's a stress reliever. When I'm out there, I don't have to answer to anybody. If I want to do something, I do it. If I don't want to do anything, I just hang out there and enjoy what I have.

My wife Lee Ann and I bought the land back in 1993. Back then that's all it was: just a rough piece of land with a beaver swamp on it. A lot of people thought we were crazy for buying it. But all they saw was what it was on the surface. To them it was just a rough piece of land that needed a lot of work before it would be worth anything. And I have to admit that in those days it was something of a mess, considering that the person we bought it from just let it go once he logged it and used it for hunting. Not long after the owner before him left, the beavers went in and built a dam, effectively turning a good part of it into a swamp. But I've always liked working with my hands. I've always liked being in the outdoors. So the work — and it was going to take a lot of it — was going to be part of the fun for me.

I saw the potential in it.

We both did. In those days, all I wanted was a place where I could plant grass and raise some cows, and when I looked at the swampy mess, that's exactly what I saw. A place I could turn into what I wanted it to be.

So I set to work. With a bulldozer I cleared off a majority of the land. Then I fenced the entire perimeter and planted grass. I broke up the beaver dam in the old swamp, drained it, and then built a new dam creating a beautiful five acre pond which we then restocked with bass and brim. A few years later a small one-room cabin was added; a place to get out of the weather and stay the weekends. Then we raised cows for a few years.

It was everything I had hoped for.

We didn't live on the farm, but we lived close enough to the property that we could take care of everything with no problem. And while cows seem to live a laid-back life, just standing in the fields watching the world go by, they still have to be checked on every few days. And I loved working with them, so on a personal level, my life was going just the way I imagined it would.

Meanwhile, on the professional side of my life, I continued to advance with the company.

By the time I turned twenty-six, I had been promoted to superintendent and had helped build a lot of different kind of projects for the company. I had been involved in everything from airport runways to golf courses. But the majority of my work was with highway projects. Blythe Construction got its first Design-Build project in 2002 (the I-85 widening in Charlotte, North Carolina from Sugar Creek to Bruton Smith Blvd.), and I was selected as the superintendent. That was quite an honor. But it also meant we would have to leave South Carolina.

While this was a great opportunity (one I couldn't possibly turn down), North Carolina was too far away to keep up the daily responsibility of caring for twenty or thirty head of cattle. So with the move in 2003 we sold the cows and decided to grow corn. So we plowed up the pasture and planted corn. That's when the idea of having a real working farm first began to take shape.

At first we just planted enough corn for our own use during hunting season. My son Sampson Jr. and I are avid hunters. Occasionally people asked me if I'd be willing to sell them some of our leftover corn, and if there was any left, I was always happy to do so. After a while the requests for corn started to increase. As more people started asking about buying corn, I began to think about growing it on a larger scale. And since we had fifty good acres available, there was no good reason not to.

I was on my way to becoming a real farmer.

Granted it's more of a hobby farm, not one we ever expected to make any money from, but it's still a farm to me. Something I had wanted since I was a teenager.

As I've said, I was raised in Kentucky, and while we weren't big-time farmers back then, we did grow most of our own food and raised a few animals. That's just how I was brought up. In fact, those early days are what started me thinking about raising cows in the first place. When I was growing up, we raised our own cows. We had a milk cow and a beef cow. We also had two or three pigs, which we slaughtered each fall.

We also had a huge garden, but didn't have a tractor. When it came time to plow a neighbor or friend would do the plowing for us with a horse pulled plow. Everything else we did by hand. We grew most of the food we ate there in the garden, and the cows and pigs provided milk, butter, and meat. Talk about organic. We were organic before organic farming became the way to grow food.

We sure did eat good back then.

Still, life wasn't all farm work. It was there in that coal mining country that I developed my love for the outdoors and my work ethic. I've always liked the outdoors. Hunting. Fishing. Just being outside, free and unconfined. The fact that I always had to work when I was younger meant hard work wasn't a chore or something I dreaded. It was just a way of life. A matter of survival.

It was a hard life, but a good life.

Thanks to a regular summer job working on a farm for three years, that's where my love of farming grew. Over thirty years later, farming is still in my blood. It's a part of my heritage. It's a part of who I am.

And on this particular day in September, it was one of the things that had me preoccupied.

We were finishing a job on I-85 up in Rowan County, North Carolina and starting a job on highway 601 in Union County, North Carolina. These are the two worst parts of any job: the very beginning and the very end. So, while we were still about six months from being completely finished on the I-85 job, I was thinking about the new 601 project and meeting with a new group of engineers and inspectors from the Department of Transportation that morning. I was especially thinking about what questions I needed to ask.

I was also figuring out how, in the midst of all the planning and scheduling, I could get my crews on 601 started, get down to the farm, pick a load of corn, and return to work. All in all, the harvesting was going to take about three hours, and I had to figure out how to do it and still get back without disrupting my regular job.

The weatherman was calling for rain all weekend, and deer hunters had been calling and saying, "Hey, we need some corn." Normally that wouldn't be a problem, but the previous weekend I had been at our company conference in Virginia, so nobody had been down at the farm to get the corn picked. Regardless, I still had a commitment to the deer hunters, and I always keep my commitments. That meant the corn had to be picked and bagged. Period.

So as I drove toward the job site, my head was buzzing with thoughts about the farm and work.

And on top of all that, I was also thinking about 9/11. It was a Tuesday morning, the same day as the original attack.

As I drove, I was listening to the Morning News on WBT out of Charlotte like I normally do. The hosts, Al Gardner and Stacey Simms, were talking about the fact that it was the sixth anniversary of the 9/11 terrorist attack on our country. At one point they started talking about the horrible images of the people who had been killed at the Twin Towers and how some people were so desperate, they had jumped out of the towers to keep from being burned alive. I remembered seeing the images on television when it happened, and as I listened to Stacey and Al, I thought it would be a terrible decision to have to make: either jump or burn to death. Little did I know that I would be forced to make a similar decision in about six hours.

I arrived at the job site still thinking about the trip to the farm. I had finally figured out how I could leave work a little early, pick a load of corn, and come back to finish out the day on the 601 project. I just had to clear it with my boss.

It's ironic that this particular workday started with two safety meetings. Each morning, on a normal day, I conduct a safety meeting for all the crews before we do anything else. We review things like how to back equipment, the proper way to get on and off equipment, and parking trucks. This morning was no exception. We had our project safety meeting just as we did every morning before we start work. It's important to remember that any time you work with heavy equipment; safety should be your first concern. I can't tell you how many times I've made that point.

Once I got the crews working I headed to the new 601 project meeting with the North Carolina Department of Transportation. This meeting opened with the topic of safety too. So on this particular day I had *two* safety meetings.

The NCDOT meeting was over around 10:30 a.m., and I told my boss, Wayne Ramsey, I needed to go to the farm to pick corn so I could beat the coming rain. I said I would try to be back around 3 p.m.

I explained to him that with the deer hunters calling me wanting corn and the weatherman calling for rain all weekend, I had few options if I planned to honor my commitments. And since the I-85 project in Rowan County was two hours away from the farm, and I would be there all week, it only made sense to head down to the farm while I was there on the 601 project because that one is only 35 minutes from the farm. If I was going to get the corn picked before the rain moved in, that would be my best chance.

Wayne knew about the farm, and he knew it had never interfered with my job, so I was hoping he wouldn't mind if I went down there for a few hours.

"Sure, that shouldn't be a problem," he said. "You're almost wrapped up here, and there won't be a lot for you to do until later this afternoon anyway, so yeah. Go ahead."

"Thanks," I said, already headed toward the truck.

"Hey, Sampson," he called out. "Be careful."

I grinned and waved to him as I drove off.

*****

I decided to eat lunch in the truck so that when I got to the farm, I could go right to work. As I ate my sandwich and drank a bottle of water, I watched the scenery slip by and allowed my mind to just drift for the first time that morning. There were soybean fields and cornfields for miles. Just the thing I needed to help me slow down mentally and relax.

Sometimes when I'm driving to the farm early on a Saturday morning, I look at the houses. Most of them are dark. Maybe one or two have a light on. Then I begin to think about the people who live there. I wonder if they are still sleeping or getting up and what their plans are for the day. I realize how blessed I am and that not everyone wakes up with something to look forward to. I love having a farm and I have worked hard for it, but it is still a blessing all the same. Some people like to hunt or fish or shop. I love being on the farm. Other people spend money on vacations, and there's not a thing wrong with that. But I spend all my vacation time and weekends out there on the farm.

Some people love things, are drawn to certain things, and they don't know why. But I do. I know exactly where my love of farming comes from.

My dad's boss, Fred Davis, owned a huge farm in Virginia, and every year from the time I was sixteen until I was eighteen, he would hire me and a couple of other guys to work on his farm during the summer. While we had a few cows back home, he had a couple of hundred head of cattle, and he grew the corn for all the animals. It was a relatively large operation, and after working there a while, I realized I wanted a farm like his someday. I loved it over there. In fact, the first time I ever drove a tractor was out there on his farm.

What I did at home was work, but when I was sitting up on that tractor seat I'd be thinking, *This is fun*. And that's what started it. Those summers on Mr. Davis's farm right across the line in Virginia. That's when I started thinking that one day I'd have a farm of my own.

And I never drive down the road to our farm that it doesn't all come back to me.

It's a part of me.

So I drove, admired the fields on either side of the road, and felt the tension drain away with every passing mile.

I arrived at the farm around 11:30 a.m. and fueled the tractor. I hooked my New Idea 323 corn picker up to the tractor and attached the corn wagon to the corn picker. Then I headed to the field.

A one-row corn picker isn't a very complicated piece of equipment. It is exactly what it sounds like it would be: a machine that picks corn one row at a time. And while it's not fancy, it beats the heck out of walking up and down the rows pulling corn by hand.

The power for the corn picker comes directly from its connection with the tractor. As you pull the picker behind a tractor, the corn stalks pass between the two gatherers and are drawn into the snapping rollers. The rollers snap the ears of corn off the stalk, and the corn is carried to the husking unit. There the machine removes the husks and silks by using a series of close-set rollers studded with husking pegs. After the husks and silks are removed, an elevating unit carries the corn up and "shoots" it into the wagon, which is pulled behind the picker. When all three pieces are hooked together it looks like a small farm equipment caravan going through the field: the tractor, the corn picker, followed by the wagon.

As I drove the tractor that morning, I kept thinking that it was a great day to pick corn. The stalks were so tall and beautiful, and the ears were so big. This was the best corn crop we'd had since we started growing corn four years earlier. In fact, there was so much corn that I had a hard time deciding on where to start. All I knew was that I didn't want Sampson Jr. to cut the corn down the ditch line because that's the most dangerous area to cut, so I finally decided that would be the best place for me to start.

While I was picking the corn — watching the ears go through the picker, listening to the shucks being ripped off the big ears of golden yellow corn and the corn going up the elevator into the wagon behind the picker — my mind started to wander. The farm was already working its magic on me. To see the corn that had started out only five months ago as seeds grow into these big ears being harvested was just awesome.

That's another reason I like farming. I know it sounds, well, corny, but it's the truth. I like watching things grow. To me, that's an incredible process.

In the spring, I love plowing the fields, planting the seeds in the ground, and then watching them come up and grow. It's just amazing. Through the summer months, I love watching the corn grow taller. And in the fall there's harvesting the corn. That's the best. It's something every farmer feels. I know a lot of farmers, and they'll all tell you the same thing. They enjoy harvesting good crops. Of course, bad crops are also a part of the cycle sometimes. It happens, and all you can do is deal with it and keep going.

But a good crop — that's where everything comes together.

As I made my way down the rows, the sound of the tractor and the rumble of the corn picker were as soothing as the sound of rain on a tin roof late at night. I had no way of knowing that very soon, that same mechanical drone would sound like something straight out of a horror movie.

After about an hour of picking, I noticed the wagon was getting full, but instead of heading back to the barn, I wanted to keep going and see if I could get just a little bit more. Sort of like a kid who says, "Just five more minutes," when it's time to go to bed. So I decided to pick one more round and then head back to work.

As I positioned the tractor on the next row, I noticed the right front tire was getting low. The last thing I needed was a flat tire, so I cut off the PTO which runs the corn picker, turned the tractor around and started toward the barn, hoping to get there before the tire went completely flat. A minute later I looked down again, and from the angle where I was sitting, it looked like the tire was about to come off the rim.

I stopped the tractor, got off, and checked the tire. It was still on the rim, but just barely. I kicked the tire and said a few things I would never hear myself say in church on Sunday. My truck was parked up at the barn, and I knew I had a small air compressor in the back. So I turned off the corn picker, walked the last hundred yards to the barn, and drove my truck back down with the air compressor.

I pulled up beside the tractor and hooked the air compressor to the tire. It is not a high-powered compressor — it's more suited for small jobs — so I figured it would take about fifteen or twenty minutes to inflate the front tire.

While I was waiting, I decided to clean off the corn picker. The tractor was still running at low idle, but I didn't cut it off because it is temperamental and had been running long enough that it would need to cool down before I turned it off. Sometimes after it has been running a long time and I turn it off, the tractor won't crank back up. So I let it continue to run to keep from having problems later.

The corn picker was an old rusty piece of farm equipment I had purchased the year before. But even a rusty old piece of farm equipment is better than picking corn by hand. Plus I was mechanically inclined enough to keep it running.

Even so, I had only used the picker for one season and it had given me problems the whole time. The corn shuck discharge chains were continually jumping off the sprockets and whenever that happened, it meant shutting the tractor down, getting down, putting the chains back on, climbing back on the tractor, restarting it, and hoping it wouldn't happen again.

But it always did.

Add to that the fact that the screen at the bottom of the picker seemed to stay clogged all the time. That problem was such a pain that I finally decided to take the chains and the screens off not long after I bought the picker. That way the shucks could just fall out onto the ground. It worked well enough, though the rollers still clogged up from time to time.

When I walked around behind the corn picker, I saw that the shucks hadn't fallen on the ground like they were supposed to. Instead, they had piled up inside the picker below the set of rollers that take the shucks off the corn.

Aggravating old used piece of *junk.*

I knelt down and started pulling out the dry corn shucks and tossing them on the ground. They were packed in there tight and I was making a big pile all around me. By the time I had removed about half the shucks, I came across a corn stalk that was jammed between a couple of rollers. I pulled on it, but it didn't budge. The stalk was sticking out of the rollers at the bottom of the picker, and no matter how hard I pulled, it refused to move. I tried to pull it through for a few more minutes, but it was stuck.

I said a few choice words and went up to see how the tire was coming along.

Unfortunately, it wasn't making much headway. The tire was only about halfway inflated. For a moment I thought about stopping everything and just driving the tractor to the barn on a half-pumped-up tire, putting the corn wagon in the barn, and just going back to work.

But I didn't.

I headed back to the corn picker to work on that stalk some more. On the way back, I reached up on the tractor and turned on the power take-off that starts the corn picker. I thought if I turned the corn picker on, it would just pull the corn stalk through the rollers and that would be the end of it. So I walked back around behind the picker, knelt down again, and saw the corn stalk was still stuck.

Without thinking, I reached inside the back of the corn picker and grabbed the corn stalk. There's an open area about six inches wide on the backside of the picker. Just enough room to reach up from the bottom and grab the corn stalk. I pulled down hard, but the corn stalk was still stuck. I re-gripped the stalk, shifted a little, and pulled down again.

Nothing.

I thought about it for a second and realized that, considering the way the rollers were moving, all I was doing when I pulled was working against them. So I changed my strategy and pushed up on the corn stalk.

That was my mistake.

CHAPTER 2

For some reason all of my safety training went right out of my head. Thanks to my annoyance with that one corn stalk, I managed to do everything wrong. And I started by doing something I would have yelled at anyone else for doing because it was so dangerous.

There's about a six-inch space at the back of the machine that runs almost the entire width just below the rollers, and without thinking, I reached in and grabbed that corn stalk and started pulling. After a few seconds I realized that wasn't going to work, so I got a better grip and pushed on it.

That's when everything changed.

The corn stalk shot up through the rollers, and in that split second, the rollers grabbed my work glove and pulled my hand into the machine. There are six rollers that work in pairs, rotating in opposite directions with less than an inch of space between each one. Three rollers are rubber and the opposite three are steel. Within seconds of the rollers grabbing my glove, my right hand was wrapped around the rubber roller going in one direction, while the steel roller rotating in the opposite direction started cutting into the glove.

And my hand.

The pain was incredible. It was like sticking my hand into an industrial meat grinder.

In a matter of seconds, the metal roller ripped through the heavy material of the glove and started cutting into the meat of my hand. The more I pulled, the more it ate away at my hand. It was all I could do to keep the rollers from pulling my whole arm up into the machine. And I knew if that happened, I was as good as dead.

At first I was stunned. Then I was mad. Then I started cussing, partially because of the pain, but mostly because of my own stupidity. I could not believe that I had done something that stupid. And the whole time I was screaming.

I wasn't thinking rationally. Random things just flashed through my mind, and for a while all I could do was keep pulling against the rollers as they continued to grind my hand to pulp.

Then I remember thinking, *My wife is going to kill me!*

Lee Ann had told me over and over to be careful working on the farm by myself, and here I go and do something this stupid. I continued to pull against the machine with all the strength I had. You would have thought I was literally trying to pull my hand off. But the more I pulled, the worse the rollers would cut into my flesh, ripping away skin, tendons, and muscle.

I had to get loose.

Or die.

I tried to think through the pain. Tried to come up with some sort of plan. I had to come up with a way to get out of this predicament. At this point, my superintendent mentality started kicking in. I needed some sort of leverage. So I gripped my right forearm with my left hand, braced my feet against the bottom of the corn picker, and got ready to pull. In that instant, I felt the first twinge of hope. I just knew my plan was going to work. It had to. I was going to pull what was left of my hand out of the rollers, wrap it up with my shirt, and drive myself to the hospital in Camden.

It sounded like a good plan. At least, I hoped it was.

I settled back and pulled with every ounce of strength I had. My legs and back strained against the picker. I put my shoulders into it, pulling against the machine, desperate to be free. But even as I pulled, the mechanism growled, and the rollers continued to pull my hand farther into the machine.

I could feel the teeth on the steel rollers as they ate through my hand and chewed down to the bone. Blood and pieces of my hand were running down my arm, and I was afraid I would pass out soon. And if that happened, I knew I was doomed to being eaten alive by this machine.

So far all my plan had done was push my hand farther into the rollers. I needed another plan. I had to do something else. In my desperation, I started yelling for help.

I think in the back of my mind, I knew it wouldn't help, but what else could I do? The problem was that the closest road was about a half mile away, and the closest house was about a mile and a half from where I was. The pine trees on our property are about 30 feet tall, so between those and the acres of corn, I was pretty much blocked from the sight of anybody who might be driving by.

Still, I screamed for help as loud as I could in the hope that someone may have pulled off on the side of the road. There is a paved pull-off area that truck drivers sometimes use to stop and take a stretch, and people use it a lot.

But nobody seemed to be using it that day.

I thought about my work phone, and then remembered it was charging in the truck. For some reason, I didn't bring my personal cell phone with me — the one we use for a house phone, and the one I take with me on the weekends. All I had was the work phone. And it really didn't matter that it was in the truck, because I couldn't get a signal on it out at the farm anyway.

I started to feel like everything was going against me.

I screamed for what seemed like hours. Screamed and pulled against the machine that growled and continued to cut away my hand, spewing chunks of flesh and blood everywhere. The mechanical sound that had always been so soothing now sounded like death.

I was starting to get tired, and I couldn't help thinking that it could be hours before anyone came looking for me. Lee Ann's job was in Salisbury, North Carolina, so she wouldn't come looking until sometime after work, and the guys at the site wouldn't think anything about my not coming back to work. They would probably think it was just taking longer than I told them it would. My son, Sampson Jr., had made plans to play softball with a local church team later that day. So it would be sometime late that night before he would think to come looking.

And nobody else knew I was out there.

I knew I was in trouble. I also knew for a fact that if I didn't get help somehow, this machine was going to kill me, and the two people who would find me would be Sampson Jr. and Lee Ann, and I was not about to let that happen if it was humanly possible. They were not going to come out to the farm and find me dead, eaten up by this machine.

I knew I couldn't pull my hand out as long as the machine was running, and since I had filled the tractor up before I started, I also knew it would be running for a long time.

I started looking around on the back of the machine, and I saw the pin that locks the picker to the hitch on the corn wagon and thought, *Yes sir, now I've got a piece of steel. That should jam the machine enough for me to pull my hand out.* I felt a rush of hope at the thought. So I took the pin and reached up and into the picker from the top side and started trying to jam the pin in the rollers, and in the process I almost got my left hand caught in the picker. In the position I was in I could not see the rollers or where to guide my hand or place the pin. Fortunately I didn't have a glove on that hand, so I felt the rollers and pulled my hand back just in time. But when I did, it caused me to release the pressure on my other hand just a little bit, and it was enough that my hand started being pulled even farther into the machine.

By now, I'd had just about all I could take. If I couldn't find a way to free myself soon, my worst nightmare was going to come true: My wife and son would find me dead in the middle of the corn field stuck in this corn picker. So I positioned my left arm against the back of the corn picker, braced my knees against the bottom of the picker and thought my only hope would be to physically pull my arm off.

I rocked back and pushed against the picker with all the strength I had left. It hurt so bad that I began to scream at the top of my lungs. I had never felt pain like that in my life … had never imagined that kind of pain … but I was in a life or death struggle, and all I could think of was my wife and son finding me dead. So I kept pulling. And screaming. I pulled until I was exhausted.

Then I sat back as best I could to rest, knowing nothing short of a miracle was going to save me.

Then, I started to pray. I called out to God. *"Please help me. God, I can't do this alone. Please help me."* And as I prayed, I started rethinking how I could get myself loose. Not reacting, but thinking with a purpose.

I realized the machine was much more powerful than I was, and instead of fighting it, I was going to have to find a way to stop it. So I started throwing dirt and rocks into the rollers hoping it would jam them and give me time to figure out how to get my hand out. But the rollers kept turning. When that didn't work I took off my boots and tried to jam one of them into the rollers, but it was too big.

At one point I thought if I threw the other boot and hit the power take-off lever, that would cut off the machine. But it would take a perfect throw to hit the lever, and that wasn't likely to happen. So I gave up on that idea and tried to jam the second boot into the rollers. Then I took off my belt, hoping to wrap it around the rollers and maybe jam them that way. I threw anything close at hand in there to try and stop the rollers.

No luck.

I had to stay focused and find a way to jam the machine.

While I was collecting myself for another attempt to get free, I looked down and saw the big hitch on the back of the corn picker. That hitch was attached with a 12 inch by 3/4 inch diameter pin. And that large pin is locked in place by a cotter pin. I knew if I could remove the cotter pin, then I could slip the big pin out, and that might provide me with a tool I could use to stop the machine.

Somehow I reached down and pinched the open end of that cotter pin together, slipped it out, and pulled the large pin free. I have since tried to do the same thing under normal circumstances and I can't physically do it. Even now it takes a pair of pliers to bend and unbend the same type of cotter pin. But that afternoon I was able to remove the cotter pin and get the big pin free from the hitch. Then I started jamming the big hitch in the top of the machine in order to try and stop those rollers.

It didn't work.

After unsuccessfully jamming the big hitch in the top of the machine I remembered that there is a series of gears and chains on the side of the machine, and that mechanism is what drives the rollers. I thought if I could jam that 12 inch pin in just the right spot, I could stop the rollers and pull my hand free.

I had to stretch, and the more I stretched, the more the machine ate away at my hand. My first attempt didn't work. In fact, the chain and gears almost snagged the fingers on my left hand, and I dropped the pin. I was frustrated and in agony. I grabbed my arm and screamed in pain. By this time I had been fighting for over an hour and a half, and the whole time blood was streaming down my arm.

I was afraid I was going to bleed to death.

Plus, I could only imagine what my mangled hand looked like. And in the midst of my frustration, I cried out to God again, *"Please help me. I don't know how much more I can take. Please, God. Help me."* I cried that prayer out over and over again as earnestly as I have ever prayed anything in my life.

After a minute, I calmed down and started thinking again. I stretched and reached around, feeling on the ground because I couldn't see where the pin had fallen. Suddenly I felt it, snatched it up, and prepared myself for another try. Though I couldn't see my ultimate target, I reached up toward the gears and was able to jam that pin between the gears, the chain, and the tire on the side of the machine. Perfect. All of a sudden, the rollers stopped.

I couldn't believe it.

Then I thought, *All I've got to do is pull my arm out of the machine, wrap it up in my t-shirt, and drive myself to hospital.* I knew my hand and part of my arm were probably destroyed, and I'm a big enough wimp that I knew I wouldn't be able to look at it.

Even so, I knew everything was going to be fine.

I gripped my arm and started pulling. I pulled and pulled, but it wouldn't move. It was stuck tight. I braced my feet against the bottom of the picker again and pulled harder, trying once again to pull my hand off. I sat back and thought about it. If my hand was already destroyed, I was going to have to do something different, since I couldn't pull it out. Maybe my glove was stuck, and that was keeping me from getting loose. So I reached in my pocket and pulled out my John Deere pocket knife, figuring I'd cut the glove away. Oddly enough, I hardly ever carry a pocket knife. Many construction workers do carry one; I just never have. But that day I slipped it in my pocket before I headed out the door. And to put things in perspective, this wasn't just any knife. It wasn't a big, heavy, lock-blade work knife. It was small (about three inches long) and had been given to me at a NASCAR race (the Charlotte Motor Speed Way All Star Race) by someone from James River Tractor, a local John Deere dealer.

Before I could get to my glove, I had to clear away all the dirt, boots, belt, and other stuff I had thrown up there to try to jam the rollers earlier.

I could feel with my free left hand that the glove was torn to pieces. I could also tell that my hand was swollen. At that point I realized it was my hand that was keeping me from getting free. My fingers were still in the rollers. I figured my only chance was to cut my fingers off. So I reached in with my knife and started cutting away my fingers. My hand was so numb that I couldn't feel it. So I cut away the first finger. Then the second one.

As I finished cutting off my third finger, I stopped. Something was wrong.

On the side of the corn picker where I had jammed the big pin there is a clutch, and it had started to slip. Occasionally I could feel the rollers move a little, and I thought, *If I don't hurry up and get this done, I'm going to be back in the same position.* To make matters worse, every time the clutch would slip, it threw off sparks. And it threw them on the dry corn shucks I had piled on the ground around me.

I smelled smoke.

Then the heat hit me like a hammer.

I had one finger and my thumb left to cut off, but before I could get started on finger number four, I was engulfed in flames. The corn shucks I was kneeling in were so dry they went up like a gasoline fire.

I was so scared. After all I had been through with the rollers, I couldn't believe what was happening. Now I not only had a trapped hand, but also a fire to deal with.

I dropped the knife in the top part of the machine where I had been cutting away my fingers and with my left hand I started pushing the burning corn shucks as far away from me as I could. But now I had a bigger problem. I could only push the shucks as far as the tire on the side of the machine. So now the tire was starting to catch on fire, and so were the dry shucks that were still clogged inside the machine. I kept pushing them away with my left hand and my right leg, and now my jeans were on fire too.

17

When I looked up from the burning shucks, I could see that my right arm was on fire. The fire was so intense that skin was dripping off my arm like melting plastic. I knew if I didn't do something fast I was going to burn to death. And in that instant I remembered the images that Al and Stacey had been talking about on the radio show earlier that day. Those people in the Twin Towers faced with the decision to either jump or burn to death. Now I faced a similar decision.

Cut my arm free or burn to death.

I started praying again. I cried out to God to help me, and almost immediately it felt like somebody took my left hand and guided it through the flames and back into the rollers. I started feeling around in the burning machine for my knife, and after a few seconds I brought it out. Without any hesitation I jammed the blade into my right arm about three inches below my elbow and started cutting the meat away from the bone. And as bad as it hurt when my hand was caught in those rollers, then catching on fire, that was nothing compared to the pain that hit me when I started cutting into my arm and hit the nerves. The pain was unlike anything I had ever felt in my life.

There are no words to describe it.

I must have passed out for a second or two at that point because I remember feeling like I was having an out-of-body experience as I looked down and saw my mom and my wife in a funeral home arguing about where I was going to be buried. Then I saw my son and his girlfriend in a church walking down the aisle dressed in wedding clothes. I wasn't there. I looked down at them thinking, Oh man … and started shaking my head. I must have shaken it for real, because suddenly I was back at the corn picker with the flames blowing all around me. I finished cutting what was left on my arm until I got to the bone, and then I started jabbing the knife blade into the bone. The whole time flames were still burning away at the remaining skin on my right arm. I continued to jab the bone with my knife, but I wasn't making any headway in cutting through the bone. There was no way that little pocket knife could do the job.

The wind shifted and blew the flames and the hot, black smoke from the tire into my face. I was in a panic. I knew at that point that the only way I could get free would be to break the bone.

At the bottom of the six-inch gap where my arm went in the machine was a thin piece of sheet metal running the length of the gap. I didn't stop to think. From the kneeling position I had been in now for close to two hours I rose up as high as I could and dropped to the ground with all my might.

The bone snapped.

The instant the bone broke, the tire exploded. It felt like somebody slapped me hard in the face, and the force of the explosion blew me back about five feet. I landed on my back and immediately jumped up and hollered, "I'm free … I'm free!"

Looking back, as bad as the fire was, if it hadn't been for the fire I would never have cut my arm off, and I might have died right there. I really don't think I would have gotten free. Even after stopping the machine and cutting off my fingers, I don't think I could have freed myself from that corn picker.

It never even crossed my mind to cut my arm off until that fire broke out. I believe God was right there with me, and it was not meant for me to die that day. I believe that with all my heart.

Despite the fact that I was finally free, I now had a more immediate problem. I needed help. I had to get to a hospital fast. I used my left hand to pat out the flames on my jeans. I knew my only chance was to get to my truck and get out to the road if I had any hope of getting some help.

While I was putting the fire out on my jeans, I ran around the tractor and back to the truck. The tractor was sitting there running and the corn picker was on fire, but right then none of that mattered. I just got in the truck; instead of pulling forward I backed up for some unknown reason, and vaguely remember wondering if I had hit something. I don't know why I put it in reverse. Probably panic. But I finally got the truck in drive and put what was left of my right arm up on the center armrest of the truck. The end of my right arm, which no longer had a hand, was shooting blood out about three feet with every heartbeat.

All I could think about was getting some help. I never took the time to try to stop the bleeding. I just wanted to get to the road and get some help. And I was so thirsty. I wanted some water so bad. I wanted some to drink and wanted some to wash my face. When I drove by the barn I saw the water hose there and I almost stopped to wash off and get a drink. But suddenly I felt like somebody was beside me telling me, "You've got to get to the road. You've got to get to the road."

I had been in a battle for my life with a corn picker for over two hours, and now I was free. The adrenaline that had sustained me through the ordeal was depleted, and I was beginning to feel the panic and shock setting in. I couldn't believe what I had just done.

I had just cut my arm off.

I drove from the corn field up to the road (Highway 521), parked on the shoulder, and tried to wave people down. Even though it was a busy road, nobody would stop. They just kept driving by. As I watched them drive by I thought, *I've got to get somebody to stop.*

The hospital was ten miles away and I knew there was no way I could make it that far on my own. How much more could I take? How could I get someone to stop? As the reality of my situation hit home, I did something I would have never done if I hadn't been so desperate.

I pulled my truck into the middle of the road, blocking both lanes and placed it in park. Then I turned on the air conditioner, leaned my seat back, and prayed. "God, I've done all I can do. I'm in your hands."

Even as I sat there in the middle of the road, people managed to drive around me onto the shoulder of the road and then kept going. I imagine people were just afraid to stop because of how bad everything looked. The inside of the truck was covered with blood. The center armrest had gone from grey to red. The windshield looked like someone had taken a water hose and sprayed blood all over it. There was so much blood, I was beginning to wonder how much I could actually have left in my body.

I was weak, but I was content. I had done all I could do. I was free, and I was in God's hands.

The next thing I knew, the door opened and a man stuck his head in and said, "Hey mister, do you need some help?" I looked at him and held up what was left of my right arm and said, "Yeah, I think I need a little help."

I will never forget his face. He jumped back, and the sweat just started pouring off his forehead. He said, "Don't move. I'm medically trained and I'm going to help you. I'll be right back." as he headed toward his car I called after him, "I'm not going anywhere."

In just a few seconds he was back with his paramedic bag. He leaned in the passenger door and put some huge gauze pads from a birthing kit on my arm. He opened one package after another, and every time he put one of the pads on me he'd tell me to hold it in place. And I did, but I never looked at my arm. At the same time he was also trying to tell the 911 operator what was happening. While he was talking to her, the superintendent in me came out. At some point he told me his name was Doug Spinks, so I said, "Doug, tell her I need a helicopter. I need a helicopter out here."

While Doug was dealing with all this, a woman looked in from the driver's side and asked if she could help. Her name was Karen Baker and she was a nurse. She said something to Doug when she first got to the truck, and he said, "He's real shocky. Just keep him calm and don't let him go to sleep."

Now here I was, out in the middle of nowhere, parked in the middle of the road, on the verge of bleeding to death, and the people who stopped to help me were medically trained professionals, a first responder and a nurse. Now if that's not God sending me help, I don't know what is. And for those people who aren't sure they believe there's a God who answers prayers, just wait. It gets better.

Doug told me later that he had left work early that day. He wasn't even supposed to be out there. In addition, he normally didn't have his paramedic bag in that particular vehicle. Then, to add to the "coincidence," Karen "just happened to come along" right behind him. She left work early that particular day because she had a doctor's appointment, and the timing had put her on the road at that exact time.

Say what you will; as far as I'm concerned, all of that is too much of a coincidence to be a coincidence.

I couldn't stop thinking of Lee Ann and asked Doug to call my father-in-law, Keith, and tell him what happened. I wanted the news of my accident to come from family. I didn't want some stranger telling Lee Ann that I'd been in an accident, so I figured it would be better if she heard it from her father. Keith is a retired Air Force Brigadier General who used to fly fighter jets, and I think growing up in a military family is one of the reasons she is such a strong woman. But even as strong as she is, this news was going to be hard enough for her to take coming from family.

Doug said he would make the call.

While he was occupied, I asked Karen for a drink of water. I told her Doug wouldn't give me any, and all she had to do was reach over on the back seat of the truck and get the water for me because I always kept a couple of bottles in my lunch cooler.

She wouldn't do it either.

"Mr. Parker, I know you're thirsty, but I can't do that. You're probably going straight to surgery once you get to the hospital, and the surgeon's going to want you to have as little in your stomach as possible."

The logic of what she was saying registered somewhere in the back of my mind, but I was still so thirsty.

The whole time she was talking to me, she was also doing everything she could to keep me calm and comfortable. "Mr. Parker, don't you worry. You're going to be OK. Pretty soon you're going to be on the helicopter, then it'll just be a few more minutes and they'll be landing at the hospital," she said. She sounded so reassuring. "So what I need for you to do right now is just keep talking to me. You've got to stay awake until they get here, OK?"

She kept talking and asking me questions, alternately comforting me and asking me questions to keep me awake. Did I remember my name? Where did I live? Did I have a family? I got my hopes up at one point when she reached back for one of the water bottles. I thought, *Great! She changed her mind.* But she hadn't. She got the water so she could wet a cloth and wipe my face. It might not have been a drink of water, but it was the next best thing, because not only did it feel nice, but every once in a while a little water would trickle down, and I'd stick out my tongue and try to catch it. I can only imagine what was in those drops of water because my face was covered with dirt and soot from the fire. But right then it was some of the best water I had ever tasted.

About ten or fifteen minutes later the ambulance arrived. When the paramedics got out of the ambulance, it was obvious that they knew Doug. I could hear Doug telling them how bad I was, and I heard them say the helicopter was on the way. They asked Karen to move, but before she gave up her place beside me, she managed to pour out some more water on my head, and a few more drops made it to my lips.

I told the paramedics all I needed was a drink. They refused too, and instead of explaining what Karen had already told me, they went right to work on me. I sensed their urgency to get me to the hospital. While they were working on me, one of the paramedics commented on what a good job Doug had done on my arm.

Once they had made a quick assessment, Doug and the paramedics got me on a stretcher and started loading me in the ambulance. I don't think they realized until right then how tall I am, and it took them a while to get me situated.

Doug told the guys he would drive the ambulance to the place where we were supposed to meet the helicopter so they could tend to me. The helicopter couldn't land at the farm, instead it would land in a designated landing site about five miles down the road.

Karen told me she would follow us to the helicopter, and she would be praying for me, and I thanked her. While they were loading me in the ambulance, I told Karen what I had left at the farm. As far as I knew, the tractor was still running and the corn picker was on fire.

At first Karen was right behind us, and then suddenly she turned around. I found out later that she had gone back to the farm. She drove down the long gravel road, and when she drove over the hill she saw both the corn field and the corn picker on fire. She immediately called the fire department, and they were there within minutes.

The fire department was able to put out the fire. They saved my tractor and corn wagon, and if it had not been for Karen, my tractor and the corn field would have been destroyed.

I learned later that the fireman checked the corn picker to see if there was any part of my hand and arm that could be reattached. All they found were the remains of burned bones, which were lying on the ground under the picker. The rubber rollers had melted in the fire, and that had freed the remaining fingers, allowing them to drop to the ground. The firemen gathered them up in a bag and took them to Kershaw Medical Center to be disposed of.

During the ambulance ride, I could hear the paramedics talking to the hospital staff. They were giving my vital signs and filling them in on what had happened. Sometime in the conversation they received the authorization to give me morphine. I will never forget the first shot of morphine as long as I live.

I was in so much pain. What was left of my right arm was throbbing, and my entire body felt beaten up. But when they gave me that first shot of morphine, it felt like a heat wave spreading from my head to my toes. And when that morphine kicked in, man, I felt the relief immediately. The feeling is hard to describe, but I knew I had never felt anything like it before.

The landing site was just a few miles down the road from the farm, and it felt like the ride only took a few seconds. When we got to the helicopter landing site, Doug pulled the ambulance in and I could hear the helicopter landing. While the paramedics were still working on me, taking my vital signs and talking to the hospital staff on the phone, I was saying, "I want to go to Charlotte. Take me to the hospital in Charlotte."

They assured me everything was going to be OK. "Don't you worry, Mr. Parker. We're going to take good care of you. Everything's going to be fine." But I still wanted to go to Charlotte. I wanted to be closer to home.

They continued to tell me everything was going to be fine while they were getting me out of the ambulance. But when they tried to put me in the helicopter, I wouldn't fit. They kept at it until I was inside, although my feet were jammed all the way to the front glass. I guess that particular helicopter wasn't made for tall people. So they pulled my legs up a little bit and we took off. The flight nurse, Marshall Higgins, was sitting just above my head, and my head was right between his knees.

There were a couple of sponge pieces, one on either side of my head. I was still conscious and still in superintendent mode. Still telling them what I wanted and where I wanted to go.

The flight nurse looked down and asked me if I was in pain. I told him

I was, so he gave me another shot of morphine. Since the paramedics had already started an IV, the morphine brought me immediate relief.

As the helicopter took off, I was lying on my back looking up at the sky. It was a beautiful day. The sky was a Carolina blue, and there were big, puffy white clouds floating across the sky. It was so beautiful that I felt like I was going to heaven.

The flight nurse was asking me questions the whole time we were in the helicopter, trying to keep me awake. "What's your name? How did you hurt your arm? Where do you live?" And somewhere in all that, I asked him a question.

"How long will it take to get to the hospital?"

He said, "ETA is ten minutes." The hospital was over an hour away if you had to drive there. The next thing I knew, it felt like they kicked in the jets and that helicopter took off like a rocket. I'm here to tell you, that was not the first time Ronnie Ashcraft had been at the controls of a helicopter. He was, as the old timers say, making that thing walk the dog. It seemed as if just a few minutes had passed before they were taking me out of the helicopter and rolling me into the operating room. I was still awake, and it was just like you see in the movies or on that old TV show, ER.

When they got me in there, they took me off the gurney and moved me onto the operating table. There was a huge bright light above me, and about ten or fifteen nurses and doctors were already at work in the room. All of them were busy doing something. It was amazing to see how organized and well-coordinated they were.

One of them started cutting my jeans off, and I remember saying, "Hey, don't cut those off. They're my favorite jeans." Someone else was cleaning the inside of my leg so they could put in an IV, and I was still worried about the one who was cutting off my favorite pair of jeans.

About that time someone else started asking me some more questions: "What is your name? Can you tell me what happened? Was anyone else involved?" Things like that. When they got to "Do you have a living will?" I said, "Man, I have come this far, I am not about to die now."

This whole time people were working on me, putting in IVs, and doing other things non-stop. They were hooking up machines, cleaning me up, taking the bandages off my arm. And in the middle of all this, someone — I don't remember if it was a doctor or a nurse — said, "Mr. Parker, we're going to take care of you. We're going to put you to sleep now, and when you wake up, you're going to feel much better."

I think I said, "OK" or "Thank you," or something like that. Then whatever they gave me started to kick in, and I was gone.

After the surgery, the decision was made to airlift me that night to the Doctors Hospital (also known as the Augusta Burn Center) in Augusta, Georgia. They were concerned about the burns at the amputation site, as well as those on my left hand and my right knee.

I found out later that the Doctors Hospital is one of the best burn centers on the east coast, and now I know why.

The weather had turned stormy in Columbia, so the helicopter pilots had to wait until it cleared up to fly me to Augusta. They considered taking me by ambulance, but with it being about a two hour trip, an ambulance would take too long and the trip would be rough on me. Finally the weather cleared a little, and the pilot and crew decided to chance it. Even though the weather was still rough, they knew they had to get me to the burn center as soon as possible.

CHAPTER 3

When my phone rang, I figured it was Sampson calling to tell me he was running a little late. We were supposed to meet at Walmart, and I was already in the parking lot waiting.

But it wasn't Sampson. It was Mom. Many years and many grandchildren ago, my mother lost her title of "Mom." Instead we all lovingly refer to her as "Grams." So I answered with her usual title.

"Hi, Grams."

There was no normal "Hi, Lee Ann, this is Grams, how are you?" kind of greeting. Instead she said, "Lee Ann, this is Mom, are you all right?"

My heart plummeted to my stomach. I didn't like the way she asked the question, and I got an eerie, sick feeling. The kind you get when you know something is terribly wrong.

I said, "What do you mean 'am I all right?' What's wrong, Mom?"

Instead of answering, she wanted to know if Sampson was at the farm. I told her he had planned to be there earlier, but he was supposed to be meeting me at Walmart. Again I asked her why and what was wrong.

She explained that my dad had gotten a call just as she walked in from work, and they thought the person who called was from the highway patrol. They said Sampson had been in some sort of accident and was being transported to the hospital in a helicopter.

The feeling got worse. I knew something terrible had happened to Sampson.

I started asking all sorts of questions. "Was he in a car accident? Is he okay? Where are they taking him?" She could only tell me that he was being transported to a hospital in Columbia, but she wasn't sure which one it was.

My mom and dad didn't know much about the Columbia hospitals. Since my father is retired military, any time they need medical service, they go to Shaw Air Force Base in Sumter, South Carolina. She said she would try to get the phone number and call me back. She called back a few minutes later and said she could not find the number in the phone book, so she and my dad were going to get in the car and head to Columbia while they tried to get more information.

She wanted me to "sit tight" until they could give me more specifics. This was my husband she was talking about, so that wasn't about to happen. Plus, I knew that my mom and dad were in a state of shock just as I was, so I decided to take charge.

Considering the fact that I didn't really know what had happened, I was pretty calm. I dialed 411 and got the numbers for both Palmetto Baptist and Richland Memorial hospitals. I called Richland Memorial first and asked for the emergency room. I explained to the nurse who answered that my parents had received a call with little to no information other than my husband had been airlifted to a hospital in Columbia. She asked me what my husband's name was so she could check to see if he had been brought there. She put me on hold, and suddenly I couldn't stay still. I started my car, pulled out of the Walmart parking lot, and headed toward home. I knew I would be on my way to Columbia in a matter of minutes, and I needed to find Sampson Jr. to let him know that his dad had been in an accident.

The emergency room nurse came back on the line and said, "I am sorry, Mrs. Parker, but there is no record of your husband being admitted in our emergency room." I thanked her and almost cut the connection. Then I remembered the TV show, ER.

Didn't the helicopter pilots call in to the trauma units while they're in flight with updates on their patients?

I asked the nurse if they had any airlift units on the way to the hospital, and she put me on hold again. It didn't take long for her to get back to me. She said there was a unit in flight to the hospital, but she didn't know who the patient was. She asked me for my cell phone number and told me she would call me as soon as the helicopter landed and they could identify the patient. I gave her my number, thankful that I just didn't accept her first answer.

I turned left off Highway 29 onto Pitts School Road and headed toward our house in Harrisburg. It was about a fifteen-minute drive. For some reason I had this urge to pull off the road, so I made a right into the Walgreen's parking lot. I drove to the back section where there were only a few cars. I slammed the gear shift into park, threw the door open, and got out of the car. I held my arms up toward the sky and cried out, "Oh God, please, please; I am not done with him yet. I love him so much!" Then I got back into my car and headed towards the house.

I wasn't sure where Sampson Jr. was, but I knew I needed to find him. I wanted him to come with me to South Carolina. I thought for a minute, then realized that his girlfriend, Heather, would know where he was. So I called her. Sure enough, she knew exactly where he was. She said he was out playing softball for a church league not far from our house.

I was driving toward the ball field when my phone rang. It was a different nurse than the one I had talked to earlier. This one was from the trauma unit. She told me who she was, where she was calling from, then asked, "Are you driving?"

When I told her yes, she asked if I could pull off the road. As I pulled over, I just knew the news was going to be bad. Why else would she ask me to pull off the side of the road? Tears welled up in my eyes and my heart was racing.

"Is my husband there?" The emotion strained my voice. Instead of answering immediately, she asked me several questions in order to be certain I was Sampson's wife.

In a calm and reassuring voice I will never forget, she told me that my husband was there and that he was stable and was being evaluated. I asked her what had happened, and she told me that the only thing they knew so far was that Sampson had been in a farming accident. When I asked her if he was going to be okay, she told me that he had sustained a severe injury to his arm, but that is all the information she had. Then she asked if I was alone. I told her I was, but that I was on my way to pick up our son. She asked if I was planning to drive to the hospital. What a dumb question. Of course I was. I didn't say that, but that was what I was thinking.

I'm glad I kept the comment to myself. As it turns out, she was simply concerned with my safety and was making it a point to let me know there was no hurry. Sampson was in good hands and being well cared for.

I thanked her for the information and closed out the call. Then I got back on the road and was at the ball field in a flash.

Had I been speeding?

Probably.

I pulled into the packed parking lot and started looking for Sampson Jr. It appeared that there was only one field being used, so I took off at a fast walk straight up to the dugout. Someone, I don't remember who, came walking up to me and asked who I needed to see. I told them I needed to speak to my son.

Sampson came out of the dugout and said, "What's up, Mom?" I looked up into his sky-blue eyes. How do I tell this boy that his dad has been in an accident and is in a trauma unit? Could I hold it together or was I going to make a fool of myself and fall to pieces?

No, I had to be strong for our boy. I said, "Sampson, you need to come with me now. Your dad has been in an accident, and we need to go to South Carolina." His whole demeanor changed from happy-go-lucky to mature and serious. He asked if his dad was okay, and I told him what I knew. He immediately went back into the dugout, told the guys his dad had been in an accident and he had to leave.

As he gathered his things, I saw several of the ball players come up to him, pat him on the back, and let him know if he needed anything to give them a call. As he rounded the corner of the dugout, I heard one young man cry out, "We will be praying for your dad, Sampson."

Columbia is about a two-hour drive from where we live so, when we got in the car, we starting talking logistics. Should we go by the house first or head directly to I-485? Sampson wanted to change his clothes, so we stopped at the house, which was on the way. It was only a matter of minutes before we were back on the road. Traffic was heavy on I-77 South, but we seemed to whiz right through it, and before we knew it, we crossed the border into South Carolina.

While I drove, we tried to figure out what could have happened, but it was all speculation. After we had been on the road a short time, my phone rang. It was my mom. She told me that she and Dad found the hospital and that Sampson was there. I already knew what she was going to tell me, but I listened, not wanting to cut her off. She said they didn't have any new information, but as soon as they knew something, she would call me back.

Even though she hadn't been able to tell us anything new, it was something of a relief to know that Mom and Dad were there.

It was getting dark and had started to rain. I needed to pay attention to the road, so Sampson Jr. answered when she called back. In the middle of the conversation, he stopped and looked over at me, his eyes wide.

"Mom, they had to amputate Dad's arm."

That was the last thing I expected to hear.

I lost it.

"What?" I was in shock. All I could say was, *"No. Oh no. Oh no."*

At that point I didn't know which was worse — the rain hitting the windshield or the tears flooding my eyes. Between the two, I couldn't see a thing.

Sampson Jr. looked at me and, in a voice much calmer than I could have mustered, said, "Mom. Mom, stop. It could have been worse. At least he's alive."

He was right. I pulled it together as much as I could. I immediately went from shock to frustration. I wanted to be there for Sampson, and here I was miles and miles away while he was lying in a hospital bed, most likely scared and in pain. I had to get to my husband … needed to get to my husband.

But getting frustrated wasn't going to change anything, and now that I was calming down somewhat, I realized that the news could have been much worse. Like Sampson Jr. had said, at least he's alive. I prayed a silent prayer as I drove: *Thank you for letting me have him for a little more time; please, please be with him. You know how much I love him.*

I held out my hand for the phone. "Let me speak to Grams."

Grams spoke in a tearful voice as she shared the devastating news.

"Lee Ann, Sampson had to cut his arm off."

She gave me what few details she had learned, and then she told me that she and Dad had been allowed to be with Sampson as they prepared him for surgery. From what she said, he was doing as well as could be expected, and she continued to tell me that they really had no idea what had happened. Only that the doctors needed to clean up Sampson's self-amputation and that they had given him a lot of medication so he was well-sedated and wasn't able to communicate with them.

"They have him connected to oxygen equipment, and he has an IV drip so the nurse can inject morphine directly into the line whenever he needs it. They are doing everything they can to make him comfortable," she said. At least that was good news: He wasn't in any pain right now.

But the bad news wasn't over.

Grams went on to tell me that he also had burns on his left hand and knee that were severe enough that the doctors wanted to have him airlifted to the Augusta Burn Center in Georgia.

"Don't you worry," she said. "We won't leave his side until they transfer him to the Burn Center.

Although she didn't have much more information, one of the nurses had told her that the surgery wouldn't take long and that it would be a good idea for someone to be in Georgia when he arrived, if possible.

Sampson Jr. and I discussed whether we should head towards Columbia or Augusta and decided it would be best if we went straight to the Burn Center in Augusta instead of trying to get to the hospital in Columbia before he was transported. We figured that by the time we drove into Columbia, his dad would already be on his way to Augusta. So we confirmed our plans with Grams and got off the interstate to get a map.

We were driving my 2004 Ford Taurus. Since none of us is really into gadgets, we had no GPS system, and neither Sampson Jr. nor I had ever been to Augusta before. I knew Georgia was west of us, but we were going to need a little more information than that. We decided not to take any chances, so we got off on the next exit with a large gas/service station.

We found a likely-looking place, got out of the car, and headed into the store. We asked if they had maps for sale. They didn't, but the clerk asked us where we were going. I explained that my husband had been in an accident, and we were on our way to the Burn Center in Augusta. The clerk had never heard of the Burn Center, but he did know that if we took I-77 towards Columbia, we would see a sign directing us to Augusta via I-20.

Well, at least that was more than we knew when we got there.

I got a bottle of water and Sampson Jr. got something to drink and a snack. We had no idea how long this trip would be, and we didn't want to stop if we didn't have to.

The rain was still coming down, and we settled in and followed the interstate signs to Augusta. It was hard not to think the worst, so Sampson and I busied ourselves by talking about who we needed to contact and how we could get their numbers. It was a time-consuming task, and it took the remainder of the trip for us to contact our friends and family. But it was the perfect chore to keep Sampson Jr. occupied during the drive.

Grams called to let us know that the helicopter wasn't able to take off due to the bad weather, and the crew was going to wait out the storm. We knew all about the storm. We were right smack in the middle of it. Add to that the fact that I don't like driving at night, much less in a storm and in unfamiliar territory, and I could only imagine the frustration the helicopter crew must be facing.

I prayed again, asking God to grant all of us safe travels.

Grams said that Sampson's surgery went well, that he was resting, and was still heavily medicated. We found out later that Sampson was so well medicated that he didn't remember my parents being there.

But they never left his side. They were there when he went into surgery, and they were there when he came out. My dad even walked beside him as they rolled the gurney out and loaded him into the helicopter. In fact, Dad told me the next day that he was a little upset at how they were manhandling Sampson. Their response was that he was medicated and could feel no pain. My dad quickly set them straight and directed them to treat him gingerly and to take good care of him. It sounded like the General had spoken. Dad can be pretty authoritative when the time calls for it.

My mom, who can be equally fierce when it comes to family, was worried about leaving the hospital without Sampson's personal belongings. She fought to have them handed over to her. She was told many times that the only person who could receive the belongings was his spouse. Somehow she was able to convince them to let her have them. She had won the battle and was very proud of her accomplishment. At the time I really didn't think much of her efforts, but later, when I got the bag with all of his belongings and emptied it out, I cried like a baby. Later, I wrote in my journal:

It's funny the things that get your emotions churning.

When my mom gave me a bag with all the things Sampson had with him when he got to the hospital, I looked in it and saw Sampson's wedding ring, watch, wallet, and some cash and loose change. I took every item out of the bag and savored the thought that I still had my husband. One of the first things that struck me was the fact that his wallet was covered with soot, as was everything inside it.

Sampson wasn't able to wear his wedding band for quite some time because he had suffered third degree burns on his left hand, and the surgeons placed cadaver skin on top of what skin was left to promote healing. He later had some of his own skin grafted onto the hand.

I cleaned up the ring and put it on a chain. I vowed to wear his ring around my neck while he was unable to wear it himself and did so until I took it to the jewelers and had it resized and polished. Sampson didn't wear it for several months, and then one day he pulled it out of his top dresser drawer and said, "I think my hand has healed enough; time to wear this ring again."

He still wears it today.

He never went back to wearing his watch. The type of watch he used to wear, a simple Timex with a leather band and an old-fashioned latch, was difficult for him to put on. I would have been more than happy to put it on for him every day, but he wanted to be as independent as possible.

We continued to make our way to Augusta through the black night and the unrelenting rain. When we got close, we called the number Grams had been given. Sampson Jr. did the talking while I drove. It was amazing how we pulled together and made it to the hospital. The directions we were given weren't very good. We didn't find the hospital until we drove in circles a couple of times and then ended up somewhere outside the city. Deep down I was scared and thought we would never find the hospital, but I never let on to Sampson Jr.

God knew we needed his help and somehow, through a series of off-the-wall turns (what some would call blind luck, but I know better), there it was.

The Doctors Hospital.

I couldn't believe it. We had actually arrived before Sampson did. We found the ICU Burn Unit and rang the bell on the door. We told the nurse who we were and that Sampson was being airlifted to the unit. She said she would check. She came back a few minutes later and told us they had gotten a call, but the helicopter was still unable to take off due to bad weather.

I was really upset with myself at that point. I started second-guessing myself and thinking I should have gone to Richland Memorial instead of heading to the Burn Center. I should be with my husband. Not standing here waiting.

Then I remembered that Mom and Dad were still there with him. I knew he was not alone and he was in good hands.

Sampson Jr. and I wandered around the hospital until we found the helicopter landing pad. We sat in the car for a while, then got back out. At one point we went back to the car and tried to rest. The noisy air/heat unit kept going on and off, and every time it did, we thought it was the helicopter coming in. By that point we were so tired that we were becoming giddy. We talked nonsense and even laughed at one point, because we sure couldn't get any rest. We still had too many unanswered questions, and we both needed to see Sampson.

Finally, Mom and Dad called. They were on their way home, and Sampson's helicopter was on the way. "Lee Ann, Sampson received superb care during the time he was in the Trauma Center," she said. "Tonight before I go to bed I'm going to thank God for the first responders, the helicopter crews, the surgical team, and especially his recovery room nurse, because I have no doubt they saved his life."

I was going to do the same thing.

We got out of the car and waited in the ICU waiting room. It was nearly midnight and we were alone.

When they rolled Sampson through the doors, I was shocked. He was such a big guy that he was half off the gurney. His face was red and swollen. He had a tube down his throat, and his eyes were closed. He looked like he had been in a fight. I didn't know what to do. Can I touch him? Should I kiss him? I gently rubbed his forehead, stood on my tiptoes, and gave him a little kiss. Sampson Jr. stood there with tears welling up in his eyes and said, "It's going to be OK, Paps. We're right here."

After our brief reunion, the flight nurse told us they needed to get him to ICU. The ICU nurse told us that she would be evaluating Sampson from head to toe to determine the extent of his burns.

Sampson Jr. and I were instructed to go down to the emergency admitting area and complete the necessary paperwork. About 15 minutes into the process, we saw a group of familiar faces peering in at us from the lobby. Sampson's brother Steve, his wife Delia, their son Colt, and Sampson's sister Joyce had arrived from York, South Carolina. It was good to see family. When Steve came up to me, I could see horror and disbelief on his face. He gave me a big, reassuring hug and said, "Don't worry. I'm here."

Delia said Steve must have hit a hundred miles an hour a few times on the way to Augusta. "The only thing that mattered was getting here. We prayed and drove like crazy all the way down here."

We stayed up the entire night as we got bits and pieces of information about Sampson's condition.

The evaluation seemed to take forever.

Finally the nurse came out and said she had good news. After a complete evaluation, it turned out that the burns on Sampson's body were not as bad as they had anticipated. She said she thought at first that his feet were severely burned. But after they cleaned his feet with a Clorox solution, they realized his feet weren't burned. They were covered in soot.

Sampson Jr. and I were finally allowed to go back to see him. The ICU unit was cold and dark. There were a lot of patients in the unit, but I was afraid to look in their rooms. The staff gave Sampson Jr. and me a crash course about burn units and the many precautions they take to protect the patients. They even asked us if we had recently been sick or had a cold. Once we answered all of the questions, they showed us how to scrub our hands and arms. Then they gave us full gowns, hats, gloves, and booties. We were completely covered with a sterile outer layer.

I was shaking inside and out, partially from the cold, cold room, but mostly in anticipation of seeing Sampson. When we walked into his room, he opened his eyes slowly. He shook his head from side to side as tears rolled down his cheeks.

I had only seen my husband cry one time, and that was when his dad died a year earlier. Little did I know that this big guy would be shedding those tears for many months to come.

Sampson couldn't talk to us because of the ventilator tube that had been inserted in his throat. It was a precaution in case they needed to put him on oxygen because the doctors didn't know how much smoke he had taken into his lungs, which could cause his lungs to collapse.

I reached over the bed and kissed him on the forehead and tried to comfort him. He continued to shake his head while he looked down at what was left of his arm. I told him I loved him and that I would be here for him. Sampson Jr. kissed his dad on the forehead and said, "It will be OK, Paps." "Paps" is his pet name for his dad. It's the one he uses when he is either in a serious or a really good mood. This was a serious "Paps," but he knew his dad liked it when he called him that.

In what seemed like only a minute, the nurse shooed us out. They wanted Sampson to rest. He would be going into surgery first thing in the morning to start the cleaning and scraping process for burns. We were fortunate because the other family members were not going to be able to see him that night.

After our brief visit, we were wound up and had nowhere to go. We sat in the ICU waiting room (which became like home after a week or more of sitting and gathering in there) and discussed all of the things that *could* have happened. It was terrible not knowing what had happened. Sampson couldn't tell us so all we had left was speculation.

At some point I was talking to Delia about our daily routines when she said "I guess you'll just have new routines now. Things change, but we change with the changes. And you're both strong. I really think Sampson can overcome this." She was right. There were many changes to come and Sampson and I ended up embracing them with positive attitudes knowing that through Christ all things as possible.

After we had exhausted the subject for the night, some of us curled up in chairs and tried to sleep. I couldn't shut my mind off. I hated knowing my husband was down the hall, through the doors, and in a room where I couldn't be with him. So I did the only thing that I thought might help.

I prayed.

I thanked God for answering my prayers. Thanked him for the fact that my husband was alive. I didn't ask why it happened. I just gave him thanks and praise.

CHAPTER 4

Lee Ann and Sampson Jr. arrived at the Burn Center late that night, but I was still in Columbia because of the bad weather. They knew I would be coming by helicopter, and both of them waited outside by the landing pad until they heard the helicopter. By that time it was very early on the morning of September 12th. As the flight crew took me out of the helicopter, Lee Ann and Sampson stopped them long enough to kiss me. The flight nurses rushed to get me in the ICU burn unit.

Through it all I was out cold. Sleeping like a baby.

The first thing I was aware of was the feeling of drifting from a deep darkness into the light. That was the anesthesia wearing off, and for the first few seconds, I was really disoriented. But I was awake enough to realize something was wrong.

Oh God, there was a breathing tube down my throat. And as I became more aware of my surroundings, I saw that there were more lines and tubes connected to different parts of my body. I tried to speak, but the tube in my throat made that impossible.

Why did they put a tube down my throat?

The only answer I could think of was that I was dying.

That had to be it. Why else would they put a tube down my throat?

My dad had died the year before, and he'd had a tube like this one down his throat for ten days. I watched him lay there for over a week, watching a machine breathe for him. Every breath in and out was regulated by a machine.

My family and I finally had to make the decision to have the tube removed. My father had always been a vital and active man, and we knew he didn't want to live like that. Not hooked up to some machine, having to rely on it for every breath. So we made what was one of the hardest decisions we'd ever had to make.

We had the breathing tube removed. He died less than a minute later.

And now I was going to die the same way.

This was the kind of thing Lee Ann and I had discussed previously. I had told her nobody should die that way. Not tied to a bed with a machine doing your breathing for you. She knew how hard it had been for me to watch my dad live and die that way, and she knew I didn't want to be in that position.

Now I was really scared. I looked around the room and saw Lee Ann sitting there. Why was she just sitting there? She more than anybody else knew I didn't want to be hooked up to that machine.

I tried to call out to her and couldn't because of the tube. I motioned for her to pull it out of my throat, but she wouldn't. I started thrashing around and tried to pull the tube out with my left hand. I could not believe I had a tube down my throat!

Lee Ann called for a nurse. The nurse rushed in, pulled my hand away from the tube, and gave me a shot to calm me down. Once the shot started to take effect, the nurse explained that I had been intubated for precautionary reasons and that I wasn't going to have to be hooked up to the breathing machine for very long. They just didn't know how much damage the fire had done to my lungs, if any, and the tube was there to give my lungs a chance to rest until they knew if there had been any damage. They had run some tests, and as soon as they had the results, the doctors would know how soon they could remove it. Her best guess based on what the preliminary tests showed was that there hadn't been any lung damage, and they could probably remove the tube that afternoon.

I can't tell you how relieved I was at that point. I still didn't like having the tube running down my throat, but at least I wasn't going to die.

Not long after receiving that news, they wheeled me into the operating room to remove the tube and to start the process of removing the devitalized tissue on all my burned areas. I had suffered third degree burns on my left hand and fingers and right arm, and fourth degree burns on my right knee.

After the tube was removed, the doctors and nurses immediately started asking me what had happened, and at this point I was anxious to tell everyone my story.

*****

Word of the accident had spread, and my family and friends started arriving at the hospital. My sister Gale drove all night from Kentucky and brought my mom with her. My brother Steve, his wife Delia, and their son Colt were there. They brought my sister Joyce with them from York, South Carolina. My father-in-law, Keith, and mother-in-law, Helen, had arrived. My boss, Brian Webb, and his wife, Sally, were also there.

Everyone wanted to see me, but I was still very weak and was in the Burn Intensive Care Unit.

It seemed like there was a constant stream of doctors and nurses coming and going. Each one of them treated me like a hero and talked constantly about what an amazing thing I had done in order to save my life. They all made it a point to tell me that they would do everything they could to make me better, and if I needed anything, all I had to do was let them know.

I told them about the one thing I really wanted. Moments later, I finally got the drink of water I had been wanting since I freed myself, but my throat was so sore from the breathing tube that I could hardly swallow.

The nurses finally started letting my family and friends come back to see me. They could only come two at a time for five minutes, and each one of them had to wear a mask and a gown so they wouldn't give me any germs. With their protective clothing on, they all looked like hospital employees. Just like the doctors and nurses that had been constantly coming by.

Every one of them had something positive to say, and I appreciated it all, but I felt bad that I had caused them to have to interrupt their lives to come out there in the first place. All because of a stupid mistake. The nicer they were, the more I hated the fact that I was the cause of their having to be there.

I told everybody who came in that I was so sorry for what I had done, and every one of them told me it was okay. Not to worry about it. But I did worry about it. And I went through the ritual with everybody who came in. I apologized and they said it was okay. They were just glad I was going to be okay.

But I was not okay.

I was angry. I was scared. And most of all, I was disgusted with myself.

Now if the situation had been reversed and I had been visiting one of them because they had been in an accident, I would not have thought twice about visiting them wherever they were, and I would have been overjoyed at the fact that they were going to be okay. And it wouldn't have been an imposition in the least. That's what friends and family do.

But this was different. I had been stupid, and they had to come out here because I ignored every safety lecture I'd ever given and almost died in the process.

I had lost my right arm.

And it still hurt.

Damn.

By now everyone had gone, and I was alone with the anger. The hurt. And the fear. The more I thought about my situation, the more disgusted I became. And when Lee Ann and Sampson Jr. came in a while later, that was the final straw. I felt like I had disappointed them more than anyone else, and everything just came out in a rush of anger and self-pity. I started saying many of the things I had been thinking.

"Look at what I've done. I've inconvenienced everybody because of my stupidity. How could I have been so stupid? This never should have happened. Look at me … I just lost my arm. What good am I with just one arm?"

It all came rushing out, and I lay there in the bed sobbing and pouring out everything that had been building up since I pushed that corn stalk.

Suddenly Sampson Jr. jumped up out of his chair, climbed onto the bed, and literally got nose to nose with me.

"Paps, listen to me. You've got to stop this right now. Yeah, you lost an arm. But you're alive, and that's what counts the most. You're *alive*."

That was a powerful moment. If my son had not done what he did right then, I believe I would have continued to lay there and stew in my misery. Suddenly the son had become the father, and the father had become the son. But it was better than any medicine they had given me so far. Better than morphine for the physical pain. It was just the thing I needed. It was the very thing I needed to hear, and it was especially powerful coming from my own son.

My son is a very strong young man physically, mentally, and spiritually. And in that moment he gave me some of his strength at the time I needed it the most.

Normally Lee Ann is quick to act, but this time she stood back and said nothing. She knows I'm not the kind of man who likes being the center of attention, and she knows me well enough that she knew what I was going through inside. But while she is quick to act when the situation calls for someone with a cool head, she was wise enough to see something else happening in that moment. I could see that she was so proud of the way Sampson Jr. took control of the situation.

After being able to do little more than ride and wait and watch, I think he needed that moment as much as I did. I've always known Jr. loves me, and I love him. But in that one act, I saw my son in a new light.

Remember earlier I said love saved my life?

By the end of the day, I had a new outlook on life. And it started in that one amazing, God-given moment. Granted, my life was going to be a lot different, but it would still be a good life. And with the love of my family and friends, I knew everything would work out.

Wednesday, September 12 … Day 2

I never expected so many people to be here so soon. By the end of the day, I was emotionally and physically exhausted. I know everyone meant well — they were all there because they care about Sampson and me — so I did my best to keep a positive attitude. But honestly, I did not feel like socializing. So many questions and so many conversations were making me uneasy. At one point I felt like I was taking on the role of hostess, letting everyone take their turn to see Sampson, when what I really wished was that they would all go home. Couldn't they see all the activity was wearing him out? Couldn't they see I wanted to be with Sampson alone? Maybe it's kind of selfish, but it's the truth — I just couldn't share it.

Sampson's boss, Brian, and his wife, Sally, were true Godsends. It was obvious that they were concerned about me. They went as far as to find a nearby hotel and booked me a room. Then Sally went to Target and bought me some underwear, sleepwear, and all the necessary toiletry items I would need so

I could shower and feel fresh for the next day. That was one of the most caring things anyone did for me during my entire stay at Doctors Hospital. Almost everyone else was only concerned with Sampson and his needs, and rightly so. But people often forget that the family in a hospital situation is under a lot of stress, and they have some important needs of their own.

I will never forget how Sally and Brian took care of me during one of the hardest days of my life.

*****

By Thursday, word of the accident had continued to spread, and now it seemed like everyone I knew wanted to see me. At least fifty people had been sitting in the waiting room.

Through it all, Lee Ann had been very patient. She let everyone that wanted to see me visit with me while she sat and waited. Finally I told my sister-in-law, Lori Kay, to tell her to come next.

When she came into the room, she hugged me and started to cry.

"Hey, Lee Ann, don't cry," I said as I held her. "Everything is going to be okay."

She held me a little longer, then straightened up and smiled at me. I haven't seen her cry since that day.

She is one tough woman.

We talked some more, then she told me that my boss, Brian Webb, and his wife, Sally, had made arrangements for a hotel room for her the night before, and they had even bought her some night clothes and all the necessary items for her to freshen up. Later I overheard them talking about it with Lee Ann as she thanked them again.

"It's just hard to believe someone would think to get me a room for the night, much less buy clothes and that sort of thing."

"Please, Lee Ann, don't mention it," Sally said. "We were happy to do it."

"Besides," Brian said, "we had so much fun in Target. At one point we were standing there in the underwear section laughing about trying to decide what sizes to get, and what kind of underwear to get."

We are blessed to have such wonderful friends. Little did we know just how true that was.

Lee Ann left a few minutes later, and people continued to visit. It was one thing to know she was just down the hall in the waiting room, but knowing she was physically gone, I felt lost.

On top of that, all the different emotions I was experiencing about what was left of my right arm and the raw ends of the nerves were driving me crazy.

I could feel my fingers, yet there were no fingers there to feel. My right hand felt like it was in a bucket of ice water, and I was squeezing so hard that water was coming out of my hand. But that was impossible. I had no right hand.

How could I be feeling something that wasn't there?

This was my first of many experiences with phantom pains. I could actually feel my right hand as if it were still attached. I could feel my fingers moving back and forth. And it was an eerie feeling … a feeling that was about to drive me crazy.

The next time my doctor came in, I told him about the pains, and he started me on a high dosage of a nerve medicine called Neurontin. It's used to help control certain types of seizures in people who have epilepsy, but it's also used to relieve the pain of postherpetic neuralgia. That's doctor language for "phantom pains."

He also said he was going to have a psychologist come by to help me deal with the phantom pains.

"I appreciate it," I told him, "but I don't need to see a psychologist. The medicine should be fine."

"Oh, but you do," he said. "And I promise you, Mr. Parker, you'll thank me later."

I thought, *That man must think I'm crazy.*

Later on, the nerves in my arm started going wild again. But this time, the feeling was completely new. This time it felt like fire was coming out of what was left of my arm. I hit the call button, and the nurse asked me what I needed.

I said, "I need more medicine please." A few minutes later she gave me a shot of morphine.

Ahhhh, that was better.

CHAPTER 5

By Friday I was really miserable. I wasn't sleeping much. What remained of my right arm was still driving me crazy, and every two hours the nurse would have to come in and give me morphine. On top of all that, I was missing Lee Ann. She had gone home to get some clean clothes and other personal items she may need for the next few days and make sure everything was situated at the house. I knew she would be coming back later in the day, but I still missed her. She has always been my rock, but over those few days, I began to realize what that really means.

Late that morning, the orderly came and took me to the operating room for the second round of removing devitalized tissue, skin, and muscle.

Working with burn patients is time consuming. You have to do things on the body's timetable and not on some set hospital schedule because the body has to heal. Plus, doing too much at one time when your body has been traumatized like mine had been could actually do more harm than good. Even knowing this, there were times when I became frustrated because I wanted this whole process to be finished.

At this point I still had an elbow, and the doctors were working hard to save it. I didn't understand why right then, but later it all made sense. But at one point the superintendent in me came out again and I said, "Go ahead and cut it off so I won't have to keep having surgeries." I couldn't help it. Every now and then I would put in my two cents worth on how I thought things ought to be done, but I knew the doctors knew what they were doing.

Because of my injuries, my right leg was wrapped up in such a way that I couldn't bend it, and my left hand and fingers were taped up because of the third degree burns. That was becoming something of an irritation, not so much because it was uncomfortable, but because I couldn't do anything for myself. And for somebody who has always been independent and used to doing whatever I want, whenever I want, needing people to do almost every little thing for me was awful.

And it wasn't just the complicated things. I had to have help with just about everything I did. Going to the bathroom, for example. That was one of the most embarrassing situations I had to face because after I finished, I had to call for a nurse to clean me up.

All I could do was just keep telling myself that one day I'd be able to go home, and then I could put this all behind me.

After that morning's cleaning and debridement session, as the nurse was wheeling me back to my room from the recovery room, we met Lee Ann. She had been looking for me and just happened to be coming down the same hallway.

I can't describe how happy I was to see her. I felt like the sun had just come up. I had missed her so much, even though she hadn't been gone that long. And I knew she probably needed a break after all she had been through. But I started to cry. I couldn't help myself. I wasn't in any more pain than usual. I was just so happy to see her and the tears … tears of joy … just poured out.

Lee Ann looked down at me and promised she wouldn't leave me again. And she didn't. From that point on, she was like a mother hen watching over her chicks. And from that point on, I felt safe.

After we returned to the room, we were given some strange news. For some reason, and to this day I'm not sure why, the doctor made the decision to release me that afternoon. Then he wanted me to come back on Monday morning for further evaluation and possibly some additional debridement.

Why would he want to release me that soon? Was it because I kept telling folks in no uncertain terms that I wanted to go home? Was it because I had been in ICU for two days, and they were packed and needed the extra bed? I had no idea.

But what I *did* know was that Lee Ann was beside herself. She knew it was too soon for me to go home. How could I be ready to go home when I couldn't even dress myself because I was still so groggy from the surgery that morning in addition to all the medication I was on? And while I was excited about the prospect of getting out of there for even a few days, Lee Ann was scared. Sensing her reluctance, I assured her that I was okay to go home. In fact, I wanted to go home. A fact I had made clear on more than one occasion.

So against her better judgment, we left around three o'clock that afternoon. I squeezed myself and a number of pillows into the front seat of her 2004 Ford Taurus and off we went. I was one happy man.

At first.

For four hours I felt every bump in the road from Augusta, Georgia to Harrisburg, North Carolina. Before we left, the doctors had given me a prescription for pain medication. We didn't make it home before I was in so much pain that I thought I was going to throw up. We stopped at a CVS pharmacy and had the prescription filled, and I took the medicine immediately. Fortunately, it didn't take long for it to kick in.

*****

The next morning, all of the family members who had been at the hospital came to the house, and I was really surprised to see that my brother, Ronnie, and his wife, Pam, had driven all the way from Flat Gap, Kentucky that day just to see me. They all wanted to make sure I was okay. And while I appreciated their coming, I was so weak I was afraid I wouldn't be very good company. Still, they had made the trip for me, so I fought the weakness as best I could and tried to be sociable. At one point while we were sitting in the living room, I lifted my right arm up to adjust the pillow it was resting on, and a thick, brown, foul-smelling liquid came running out of the top part of the bandage. This scared me, Lee Ann, and even my sister, Gale, and she's a nurse. After a couple of phone calls to Doctors Hospital and a visit to the pharmacist, my arm was packed and rewrapped and everything was fine. Even so, I felt bad about having something like that happen during their visit. Finally, toward the end of the day, Lee Ann explained to my family as tactfully as she could, that they needed to find accommodations for the night. I think they were planning to camp out at the house, but the mother hen was watching over her big chick. Fortunately they all took the hint, told me goodbye, and left.

I never knew a bed could feel so good. I took my pain medicine, fell asleep almost immediately, and slept like a baby. Nobody came in at all hours to take my blood pressure and temperature. And best of all, Lee Ann was right beside me. In fact, I was sleeping so well that she was finally able to get some rest.

Sunday, however, was a different story.

When I woke up Sunday morning, I was in so much pain I didn't know what part hurt the worst. I was miserable. I didn't want to get out of bed, but then again, I didn't have a choice. I had to go to the bathroom. And just like in the hospital, when I finished, I had to get Lee Ann to clean me up. Though we had been married many years and had many intimate times together, there are just some things that should remain private, and this was one of them. But what was the alternative? My only hand was bandaged and taped. My right leg was bandaged in such a way that I couldn't straighten it out, and the toilet area of our bathroom is not large enough for me to sit down with a straight leg.

At that point our relationship reached a whole new level. Having my wife clean me up after I used the bathroom was a hundred times worse than having to call the nurse to do it while I was in the hospital (though I'm sure if she had a choice there were things she would rather have been doing too). Even so, she cleaned me up, helped me back to our bed, and brought me some pain medicine. I was feeling so sick, but tried to hide it from Lee Ann. Then, when the medicine kicked in, I went to sleep and it wasn't an issue any more.

Lee Ann and Sampson Jr. decided they wanted to go to church since I was going to be sleeping for a while, so they asked our neighbor, Bill Bloodsworth, if he would mind sitting with me until they got back. When I awoke, I found Bill reading a book in our living room. Bill is a retired safety director for a trucking company, and he loves to read. He and his wife, Jennie, live across the street from us — wonderful neighbors and great people all around.

I got up and made it to the living room to talk to Bill. He had heard bits and pieces about what had happened out on the farm, and he was anxious to hear my story. So I told him everything. He sat there, eyes wide, and listened to every word. He just couldn't believe it. By that point I was finally beginning to realize what a big deal it was.

When Lee Ann and Jr. returned from church, she fixed lunch for us. While we were eating, I realized I couldn't hide it any longer. I was in terrible pain and felt sick in a way I'd never felt before. Something was really wrong.

She called my doctor in Augusta and explained my situation to the nurse, who assured her she would talk to the doctor and call us right back. Five minutes later she called and told Lee Ann to bring me back to the hospital. They would have a room ready for me on the fourth floor burn unit.

We left within the hour. A week earlier I'd never even seen Augusta, and now within just a couple of days, I was making my second trip. But I wasn't excited about it.

After a quick discussion, it was decided that Sampson Jr. should stay home so he wouldn't miss class on Monday. He had just started his freshman semester at UNC Charlotte. He wanted to come with us, but he knew he needed to stay focused on school. From the very first day of my accident he stepped up to the plate and had become the man of the house. He was doing a great job, and I was so proud of him.

I still am.

He had been very strong throughout the whole ordeal, especially that first night when he and Lee Ann got the news about my accident. He'd been a real source of comfort and strength for Lee Ann from the very beginning and had taken on a lot emotionally, especially for an eighteen-year-old young man. But the worst seemed to be over, and his studies were the priority now.

We arrived at the hospital four hours later. The nurses took me out of the car and straight to my room. They started an IV the minute I was settled and connected me to several different monitors so they could keep an eye on my status. The whole time they were working on me, my arm was going crazy. This was worse than the phantom pains earlier. Much worse. I asked for pain medicine, and the nurse gave me the morphine directly through my IV. I knew from previous experience that the morphine would only last for a little while, but I was determined to go as long as I could before asking for more. Even so, I didn't have to say anything because the nurses knew I was in pain.

My blood pressure was sky high.

Lee Ann wasn't allowed to stay with me that night. And even though I felt better when she was around, I knew she was exhausted and needed rest as much as I did. She left my room early in the evening to find a hotel room nearby. She had worked so hard all day keeping me calm and comfortable, and I know she was worn out.

After she left, things really started to get interesting.

I was on the fourth floor, which is used strictly for burn patients. It was my first time there, and I was sharing a room with an older man who had burned his feet. He dropped a pot of boiling water on himself while making spaghetti. I can only imagine how bad that hurt. And while I could sympathize with him about the pain part, this guy was loud, angry, and mean to the nurses. He was so loud; I got scared a couple of times. I had no right arm, my left hand and right leg was bandaged, I could hardly move, and my body was covered with bruises. Basically, every muscle in my body cried out in pain, and all I could do was throw a little morphine at it when I could. I had already been through one fight with a renegade corn picker, and now I had no way to defended myself if this nut really started acting up.

So I just lay there listening to this guy complain and cuss at the nurses. Everything seemed to set him off, and once he got started, it seemed like he would never wind down. It got so bad that every time a nurse came in, I would ask to be moved to another room. I even told the nurses I would pay extra to have a different room. Wasn't there anything they could do?

I didn't have any luck, and I'm sure by that time we were both driving the nurses crazy. Finally one nurse reached her limit. She'd had enough and told him if he didn't settle down and stop all the yelling and cussing, they were going to remove him from the hospital. That got his attention, at least temporarily. He calmed down and acted civil for a little while.

Later that evening, he got up and pulled something out from under his bed. I couldn't see clearly what he was doing because of the curtain between the beds, but I could hear him getting something out of a paper bag, and then putting it back in. It sounded to me like he was pulling a bottle of liquor out of a bag and taking drinks.

That was without a doubt the worst night of my entire stay at the Burn

Center. I was sick and weak, and to make matters worse, my arm was still driving me crazy. The creepy sensations were worse than ever.

As the night progressed, I got worse and my roommate started getting louder. At one point I realized the shift change had started, and that meant new nurses. Maybe someone fresh would put a lid on the nut in the next bed.

The head nurse on the floor that night was a petite, soft spoken lady. I was hoping we would have a male nurse to keep my neighbor straight. Someone like the medical profession's equivalent of Hulk Hogan.

Instead, we must have been assigned the smallest nurse on the floor, and she was swamped. Every time she came into the room, someone would call her and she would have to leave right away. When she did, the guy would get out of bed and go straight to his bag.

By this time I'd had all I could take. My arm felt like there were thousands of worms crawling around inside of it. I started taking the bandage off so I could get the worms out. And when my neighbor wasn't digging in his bag and doing whatever else he was doing, he was cussing and yelling.

Between the worms and the nut in the next bed, my patience officially ran out.

"Hey," I yelled at him. "Will you just shut up? I have had to listen to you all night, and I have had enough of you. Now just shut up and go to sleep."

In the movies that would have been enough to make him see the error of his ways, apologize, and drift off peacefully to sleep. But in the real world, all it did was make him mad. To be fair, though, by this point I may have been hallucinating because it turns out I had a serious blood infection and it could have been partly due to the sheer amount of medicine they had me on.

He got out of his bed, his face the color of pickled beets, and came after me. In the process of getting out of bed, he ripped out his IV and blood started flying. It was messy, but fortunately it also made the alarm go off as he fell onto the floor.

I still had no way to protect myself. All I could do was scream and push the emergency call button.

It took a long time for anyone to get to the room, and in the meantime, he was bleeding all over the place as he tried to crawl over to my bed.

The first nurse to come into the room saw a bloody man crawling along the floor toward a screaming, one-armed man, and she immediately called for help. We must have looked like something straight out of a horror movie. Within seconds, three more nurses rushed in and struggled to get my roommate under control. By the time they put him into his bed, I think I was babbling a little. I told them that he was drinking liquor and that he had it hidden under his bed.

That got their attention.

They checked under his bed and they found something, alright.

A bag of candy.

That explained his problem. My roommate had diabetes, and he had been eating the candy that his friend had slipped under the bed for him. So they started giving him the proper medicine to get his sugar levels under control.

By that point I had pretty much lost it. I was so upset I started screaming at the head nurse to get me out of that room. She said she would try to get me reassigned. Then she gave me some more pain medicine.

My diabetic roommate had fallen asleep, but not me. My right arm was going wild. The worms were eating away what was left of my elbow, and I felt every bite. Their teeth were hot and terrible. And on top of that, the phantom pains were getting worse. I could feel my hand and fingers burning.

I started ripping the bandages off my right arm again to get to those worms. I was in unimaginable pain, and no one was helping me.

This went on for what seemed like hours. It was unrelenting — the worms, the hand that wasn't there. And it all hurt so bad. The nurse came into the room and caught me tearing into my arm. I was all but crying, and I begged her to cut my arm off because the worms were eating away what was left. She reapplied the bandage to my arm and taped it down so I couldn't get to it and then she tried to comfort me. She said I was scheduled to be the first to go to the operating room in the morning. I asked her what time I was scheduled to go in, and she said, "Six o'clock."

God, that was forever from now.

It was the worst night of my life.

Several times I thought to myself, *Why did I cut my arm off? I should have just given up. If I had known I was going to be in this much misery, it would have been better to give up the fight and just burn to death.*

After thinking that way for a while, I tried to focus on how God had reached down to help me. On how fortunate I was to be alive. I tried to focus on the positive, but nothing worked. It felt like the devil was out to get me.

And he almost did.

I kept dwelling on the negative. I couldn't believe everything that was happening to me. The morphine didn't stop the pain, and the worms were ravenous, eating more of my arm. I could feel the blood running out of what was left of my arm. I was so sick and all I wanted to do was get my left hand loose. I became so agitated that I dropped my call button and couldn't use it to contact the nurse, so I started screaming for someone to help me. In a case of "turnabout is fair play," my roommate woke up and told me to shut up. I told him I had dropped my call button and was in a bad way. Then I asked him to call for a nurse from his call button.

By this time it is Monday morning, and there was a different nurse on duty. When she came in, I told her I was supposed to go to the operating room at six that morning to have my arm cut off because worms were eating it away. She told me that I wasn't scheduled for surgery until 9:30 a.m.

What? Was she kidding? I couldn't believe it!

They had been telling me for three hours that I was going to surgery at 6 a.m., and now they were telling me I had to *wait another three and a half hours*. I was furious. Then a combination of anger, pride, and frustration came rushing out.

"When I first came to this hospital, you people treated me like a hero because of what I had done to save my life. You all said you'd take good care of me. And what happens? All night long worms have been eating away the rest of my arm, and blood has been pouring out of my arm, and not one of you has done anything to help me. And if that's the best you can do, I want to go home."

About the time the nurse was getting the worst of my tirade, Lee Ann walked in, and I immediately started telling her all about what had been going on. I asked her to take the tape off my left hand, but she wouldn't. Even though I was agitated, she knew something was terribly wrong. She sat with me and tried to calm me down. After about an hour of dealing with me she left the room and said she would be right back. Her gut was telling her that she wasn't going to be able to handle me much longer. She was determined to get someone to take this seriously and get me some help.

While she was out, I somehow got my left hand loose and was getting out of the bed when my brother Steve walks in. Lee Ann was relieved. She pleaded with him to get me under control and to calm me down. He didn't hesitate. He just picked me up and put me back into the bed. I was so mad it took everything he could do to keep me in bed. I had had enough. I told Steve to get me out of there. Then I told him about the worms eating my arm, and how nobody wanted to help me. By then my arm felt like it was bleeding in a bucket of ice.

My roommate told Steve I was a crazy man and I kept him up all night. Talk about the pot calling the kettle black. I told Steve that was a lie and that my roommate had been drinking.

I'm pretty sure Steve felt like a ping-pong ball.

Lee Ann had managed to get the medical staff's attention because several nurses came in and taped my left hand down again, and gave me a shot. That one must have been a doozy because when I woke up; I had already been in surgery and was in a private room. Lee Ann was sitting beside the bed, and I had a number of new IV lines through which they were giving me blood.

With the third surgery, they continued to remove dead tissue, skin, and muscle. They also engrafted cadaver skin to help speed up the healing process. A blood test taken before surgery revealed that I had a serious blood infection. This is why I had been experiencing all those horrible thoughts and feelings throughout the night.

The doctors started me on the strongest antibiotic they could give me and began replacing the blood I had lost. They ultimately gave me six units of blood.

Between the infection and losing about half of my blood, it was no wonder I had gone crazy the night before.

Later that day, my doctor told Lee Ann that he had no idea of the severity of trauma I had been through or the toll it had taken on my body. He also admitted that they should not have let me go home when they did.

After two days of antibiotics, I started feeling better. The discomfort was manageable, and I was in my right mind again. Lee Ann was there with me, taking care of everything I needed. And I can't say enough about the nurses. They were the best.

The doctors were continuing to try to save my elbow, although we were losing the battle as the tissue around my elbow continued to die due to the damage caused by the burns. And as much as I appreciated their efforts, I was getting tired of surgeries. Then they came to us with news that really made me reevaluate where I was in this whole process.

The doctor came in and told Lee Ann and me that they were thinking of putting my elbow inside my stomach in an effort to save my elbow. The procedure was based on the theory that the fatty membrane in the belly, called the omentum, has some amazing health benefits. Supposedly, the omentum, which covers most of the abdominal organs, may be helpful in keeping transplant patients' bodies from rejecting new organs and could also be beneficial in tissue healing and regeneration. That was the part that the doctor felt might help save my elbow.

The problem was, if we went this route, I could be in the hospital four more weeks. That was a shock, to say the least. But if it could be done successfully, it might be worth going through the procedure.

"What are the chances of this procedure actually working?" I asked.

"You want the truth? If we have any hope of saving the elbow, this procedure is our last option, and the chances are about fifty-fifty."

Fifty-fifty? That's it? No way, I thought.

Lee Ann and I discussed the time, money, and effort this procedure was going to require, and I just couldn't imagine another four weeks in the hospital and all the additional surgeries I would have to endure. In my mind, I knew I would not go through with the procedure. By that time I was so thankful to be alive that losing my elbow seemed minor.

I was taken into surgery for more debriding and for Dr. Hassan to make his final evaluation as to whether or not the tissue had stopped dying. During the surgery he took a break and came out to talk to Lee Ann, who was in the surgical waiting room. He told her that it didn't look good for saving the elbow. He explained that too much of the tissue, skin, and muscle had died around the elbow to allow it to remain.

It was time to make the decision between the procedure that may regenerate tissue or an amputation to remove the elbow.

He asked her if she wanted to make the decision, or give me the opportunity to make the final decision. She and I had already talked about it and she knew I would not be happy if I woke up knowing that I had to go through another surgery the next day.

She told Dr. Hassan to remove the elbow.

When I woke up from surgery, I was thankful Lee Ann made the decision to have the elbow removed. *Thank God,* I thought. Soon I would be able to go home and shortly after that, go back to work.

Three days later, I was back in surgery for more debridement, more cadaver skin, and an intermediate closure. This was becoming routine.

*****

Sunday, September 23 … Day 13

"This is the day the Lord has made; I will rejoice and be glad in it!"
– Psalm 118:24

It has been twelve days since Sampson's accident and I am beginning to wonder how much longer I will be able to keep my emotions tucked away so that I can be strong for Sampson. My birthday is coming up on the 27th and my sister, Lori Kay, and I went to Target. She wanted me to pick out a couple of things for my birthday. I was drawn to the idea of keeping a journal and we found the sweetest pink ribbon-wrapped journal and a set of multicolored pens to use with it. This was to be my saving grace, so I thought. I was determined to journal each day's feelings, thoughts and frustrations. I had heard from others that journaling was a healthy tool when facing hard times. I had also been told some years ago that if you don't want it known then don't write it down. I am a very private person and keep my deepest thoughts and emotions to myself. This will be a challenge, but worth a try. Too many days have passed to start from the beginning and so many details are a distant memory so I will start with today.

The previous twelve days, have come and gone in a haze of emotions clouded by tiredness. I am really, really tired. I am tired of this hospital, tired of not knowing if I will be sleeping here with Sampson or sleeping in a motel room, just plane tired of this whole ordeal. This tiredness is one I am not familiar with. Must be all these emotions running rampant. I battle every day to keep the negative thoughts out of my head. All the "what ifs and how comes and what will we do now?" thoughts. So enough about me. Sampson has had a good day and has felt little pain. He has been eating well and enjoying the visits from family. Earlier today he walked three laps around 4 West and took a wheelchair ride outside. He enjoyed sitting under a shade tree for about an hour. He misses being outside.

He needed a nap after all his activity. And though I know he enjoys spending time with family and friends, it is exhausting … for both of us.

Being with my sister, Lori Kay, is different. I can really relax with her. We went to dinner at Chili's, just the two of us. I love my sister, but I can't wait to go out to eat with my husband. I really miss being with him the way we used to be with each other. Will it ever be the same as it was? I fight back the tears and remember all that he went through just so that he could be here with me.

After dinner I took a shower and went back to the hospital. I felt revived and ready to spend the evening with Sampson. I took Sampson for a nice walk outside under an almost full moon. What we called it a wheelchair cruise. We spent an awesome evening moon gazing and shared a sweet kiss. Thank you, God!

*****

Monday, September 24 … Day 14

"If you want to lift yourself up, lift up someone else."
— *Booker T. Washington*

The best way to describe today is "still." Today's room wasn't a private room, but no one was occupying the other bed. I pulled the bed over next to Sampson's and we slept side by side. It wasn't quite like home, we weren't touching but we were together. Now and then I would reach over and just touch him. I longed to be snuggled under his arm and to feel safe, but it was my turn to make him feel that way. Can I do this? I wasn't too sure. I fell asleep in prayer. Praying that

God would give me the strength to do what I needed to do for my husband. We both awoke around three in the morning thinking it was our 5 a.m. wakeup time. We both rested well. Sampson ate two doughnuts, drank two cups of coffee, and then we walked several laps around 4 West. After breakfast we had a visitor. I took this opportunity to get away for a bit and recharge myself. I don't know what I would do if I didn't have a break now and then. I am thankful for visitors. Even though their purpose isn't "me" on the backend it allows me the much needed time to regroup for Sampson. I went to the Days Inn to wash clothes, hit the snack shop, shower, and get ready for the day. While I was away, Sampson had an opportunity to tell his story again.

This time he remembered several more details, like a particular period of time when he laid back with his hand jammed in the machine and yelled at the top of his lungs over and over again, "Help, help, help!" The visit was exhausting, most likely from his reliving his story all over again.

Today was also bath day. Sampson was very weak and that made things difficult. Keep in mind that he is 6'3" and I am 5'4". I never thought I would be bathing him and at this point he wasn't a big strong guy that could help me out. The bathroom was small and Sampson was feeling light headed. It took all I could do to hold on to him. Why was I doing this? Why weren't the nurses doing this instead of me? I was angry on one hand, but knew Sampson needed me to do this for him, time to pull out that Godly gift of patience and put it to use. On the next bath day, we'll leave the door open for better air circulation. Today on our walk we found a scale. Sampson is down from 200 lbs. to 187 lbs. Dad said this was Sampson's "fighting weight." I didn't dare get on the scale. I knew I wasn't at my fighting weight. Hospital food, vending machines, and slipping back into bad eating habits were putting on the pounds. I can't focus on me right now. I need to be here to support and care for Sampson. I will deal with me latter.

Sampson was able to go with me to the cafeteria for lunch today. It meant a lot not to have to eat alone. It meant even more to be able to eat with my husband. We went back to the room, and he spent the rest of the afternoon sleeping and resting.

Tomorrow we face surgery number six. The doctors plan to close the wound and perform a number of skin grafts.

I love my husband! Thank you, God!

*****

Tuesday, September 25 … Day 15.

Surgery number six.

They took Sampson in to graft skin and close the wound on his right arm. Thank God everything went well. They grafted skin from his right thigh to his knee and right arm, and to the fingers on his left hand. What wonderful news that they were able to finish up everything. Dad came and stayed with me during Sampson's surgery. At this point the number of visitors Sampson is getting has scaled back. I knew Dad's trip here today was two-fold. Of course he was here for Sampson, but most of all I felt he came to support me. I need this support. I am wearing down. I need to go home. I want things to get back to normal. I just want to cry, but end up holding the tears back. Having my dad by my side today gave me a sense of peace and security that only dads can provide. Once we knew how successful everything had been, we sat under the oak trees in front of the hospital and made calls to the family to share the news. Once we finished, Dad and I had lunch in the cafeteria. Sampson spent the rest of the day recovering from surgery.

He did really well. He seems to pop right back like he's getting the hang of this surgery thing. He wasn't in much pain before going to surgery, nor did he seem anxious. He continues to be positive and strong.

Thank you, God, for my husband, Sampson.

*****

Wednesday, September 26 … Day 16

Today I have felt so alone. Sampson has spent most of his day in "La La Land." This morning at 6 o'clock, Brenda removed the dressing from the donor site, where they had grafted the skin. It was a very painful experience. In fact, Sampson said it was worse than anything he's been through up to now, including cutting off his arm. I just can't imagine it.

I am glad I wasn't there for this ordeal. Anytime the nurses have to do anything with Sampson's arm I leave the room. The nurses give me fair warning and are honest. They have warned me that the wound is pretty gruesome. I have chosen not to look at his arm or his burns. I just can't do it. I don't have a weak stomach but I just can't bear to physically see the trauma to his body. If it's not necessary why put myself through it? I need to remain positive and strong for Sampson and not looking at his wounds has helped me remain this way. The graft site is pretty large. It covers the front and outer thigh area from above the knee to just below his pelvis, and is about six inches wide.

Sampson had to stay in bed all day in order to start the healing process for the donor site. He was restless and uncomfortable, especially when the next nurse came in late. That meant all his meds would be off schedule.

I left today for a couple of hours after lunch and went to my room and slept. Sampson wore me out with all his pain and complaining. I needed to get away. It is hard being positive all the time.

Sampson requested a lot of medication today because of the pain, so he was "out of it" most of the day. The Ativan makes his eyes roll back into his head and makes him very sluggish. I don't like to see him that way! He reminded me about how hard it was to lay in bed all day and not move. I know it must be but, I worry about him getting hooked on all this pain medication that is so freely given to him. What is going to happen when we get home? I am afraid to think about it.

I hope tomorrow will promise more movement, less pain, and healing.

I love my husband!

It looks like I won't be able to stay with him tonight. He's not happy about that at all. He told Brenda that every night is a special night when it is spent with me. Now I feel guilty for giving him such a hard time about all that pain medicine.

Sigh …

*****

I had forgotten about my doctor telling me he wanted me to see a psychologist. Since my readmission and the hell I'd gone through because of the blood infection, my thinking had been scrambled for a while, but I was feeling better now. So when the doctor came by and told me again that he wanted me to see a psychologist, I thought he was just having a little fun with me.

Later that day, a very attractive woman came in the room and said she was a psychologist. She told me that my doctor had arranged for her to meet with me. While she was introducing herself, I thought, "Man, she can't be a psychologist. She's too good looking. " And before you get the wrong idea, I love my wife, and there is nobody else in the world for me. But let's be real here. I only had an arm amputated. I wasn't dead.

The whole time she asked me questions, I kept thinking my doctor had to be playing a trick on me. This woman looked more like a beauty queen than a psychologist. And she sure didn't look at all like the psychologists you see in the movies. You know the type I mean. An older guy dressed in an old tweed jacket with hair that looks like he combed it with a leaf blower.

And that sure wasn't who my doctor sent.

She continued to ask questions, and whenever I spoke, she wrote down everything I said. Looking back, that was probably a bad thing. The more I answered, the faster she wrote. I figured if my doctor was going to play a joke on me, I'd play along. So every time she asked a question, I told her all kinds of crazy things. Man, I was having a blast.

Looking back, that was probably a bad thing too.

Later, when my doctor came back in to see me, he asked how I liked the psychologist. I said, "Man that was a good joke. I don't know who she was, but she was beautiful."

"Sampson, I hate to tell you this, but the joke is on you. She really is a psychologist."

Well, how was I supposed to know? I'd never been in the hospital for cutting my arm off before. And to make it worse, the joke really was on me because I never got to see her again. Instead, after our first (and only) session, I was assigned to her boss, the head psychologist.

The guy from the movies.

And I guess I really must have come off as crazy with the first psychologist, because her boss drilled me with some really "way out there" questions.

CHAPTER 6

During my time in the hospital I had dozens of visits from family members and friends from all over, including our good friend Dale Hall. At the time Dale was a Colonel in the South Carolina National Guard, he has since retired. We both lived in Logoff, South Carolina and had been friends for many years. Our sons, Jon and Sampson Jr., played baseball together. As a matter of fact, Dale and I, along with another good friend Tim Caraway, coached one of their baseball teams together. Tim's son, Josh, even played on the team. Our families spent many happy days at the farm fishing, hunting, and having cookouts. We even took some of our family vacations together. So I wasn't surprised to see him when he came by to visit me after the accident.

What did surprise me, however, was the outcome of our conversation.

Dale wanted to know how I was coming along and then, like most of the people who came by to visit, he asked me how the accident happened. So, like I had done so many times already, I started from the beginning.

When I came to the part in the story about the two people who stopped to help me after I parked my truck in the middle of the road, I mentioned to Dale that the man who stopped was also a National Guardsman named Spinks.

"I wish I knew how to get in touch with him," I said, "because I'd really like to thank him properly for everything he did for me."

Dale thought for a moment. "Spinks ... do you mean Doug Spinks?" he asked. "I know him, Sampson. Hang on a minute and I'll track him down."

The next thing I knew, he was calling to get Doug's phone number for me. And a few minutes after that, we were talking to Doug. I couldn't believe it. One of my really good friends was the boss of the man who helped save my life. I guess it really is a small world.

*****

The day of my final surgery had arrived. I couldn't wait to get it over with. My doctor came in and briefed me on what he planned to do. He told me he was going to remove the remaining dead tissue and close up the flap at the end of my arm. He was also going to remove a strip of skin about six inches wide and nine inches long from my right leg to use as a graft for my burns. That night, I was hurting. Once again I was tormented by phantom pains. I could feel my right fingers and hand, but when I looked down to where I thought they would be, there was nothing. What a weird feeling to have an arm for forty-five years, and then it's gone. I knew it would take time to get over the loss, but I was still worried about the phantom pains. I prayed and asked God to help the doctors do a good job the next day on my arm, and for the phantom pains to go away. Later, the nurse came in to check me, and I asked for a shot of morphine. The shot brought me enough relief to allow me to sleep.

I awoke ready to be done with the surgery. Lee Ann was right there with me as she had been through the whole ordeal. Her dad drove in from Camden that morning to be with her and to check on me. As they wheeled me down to the prep room I couldn't help thinking that this would be the sixth and hopefully the last one. I was getting pretty tired of the routine — nothing to drink or eat the night before the surgery. It never changed. And I would always be so thirsty up until they put me to sleep. The kind of thirsty I was at the farm on the day of my accident. I would ask for water, no one would bring me any.

This time while I was in the surgical prep room, the guy beside me got a drink of water. I told him he shouldn't, but it was too late. That was about the same time the nurse came in and caught him drinking water from a cup that someone had left in the room. She was so mad that she told him they would have to cancel his surgery, and wheeled him straight back to his room.

They are serious about no drinking before surgery.

She came back into the room and asked if I had anything to drink. I said, "Definitely not." Then the doctor put me to sleep and, as with the previous surgeries, I was out in a matter of seconds. Then I woke in the recovery room, and it took a little while to figure out what was going on.

This final surgery was successful. My doctor had removed the last of the dead, burned tissue from my arm, closed the end of my arm, and applied the skin graft. They applied grafts to my three fingers and the area above my right knee with the skin from my right leg.

When they took me back to the fourth floor, I found a new roommate. And once again, the pairing was less than ideal. This guy liked to talk, while all I wanted to do was rest. He started telling me his story about the spider bites on his leg. He had been bitten twice on the same leg within a couple years. His leg had a big hole in it from the most recent bite. The tissue was black around the area. They came in and took him to surgery. Later when he returned from surgery, he began talking away. Finally, he took a breath and asked me what I was in for. He was shocked when I told him my story. Shocked and a little quiet.

Later that day, he was released.

Lee Ann and I were talking about how bad a spider bite can be when a nurse brought another young man into my room. And he had also been bitten by a spider.

What were the odds?

We couldn't believe it — two roommates on the same day, both of whom had suffered brown recluse spider bites. The young man had been treating his bite himself until it got so bad that his mom finally made him go to the doctor. His leg was black, and the tissue was rotting just like the other guy's had been.

About that time we developed a momentary phobia, and we started looking around the room for spiders.

Later my doctor and a physical therapist came in and checked on me and told me I needed to start walking to help build my strength so I could go home. As soon as he left the room, I was out of the bed and down the hall. I went with Lee Ann and the physical therapist who held on to me, keeping me balanced. I was weak, but I was also determined to go home so that I could get back to work and back to the farm.

*****

Lee Ann's birthday came while I was in the hospital and to help celebrate our friends Terri Carraway and Shelia Hall surprised her with a visit, a cake and some gifts. Her sister, Lori Kay, also surprised her and came to the hospital before she went to work. They had a cup of coffee, and Lori Kay brought her a gift. While they were gone, one of my nurses, Brenda, went out and bought a birthday card for me to give to Lee Ann. And because I was right handed … used to be right handed … she had to help me sign the card. Other than Lee Ann, she too was a big help during those strange weeks while I was adjusting to things in the hospital. One night she even brought me my favorite Friday night meal: Mexican food. And while I was happy that she was able to help me do some things that were important to me, like making sure Lee Ann had a birthday card (plus bringing me some great Mexican food), I was also a little sad.

You see, I've never been one to be waited on. I've always been independent. Able to do whatever I set my mind to. And now here I was lying flat on my back, having to rely on other people to do almost everything for me.

I hated that.

*****

Thursday, September 27 … Day 17
"Holding it together when everyone else would give up is true strength."
– hunting show

Happy Birthday to me! I'm 51 years old today, and this is the most special birthday ever because my husband is alive to share it with me. True strength and the grace of God gave me this awesome gift. Thank you, God! My day started out with a surprise early visit from my sister, Lori Kay. We had coffee and enjoyed the morning together. My youngest sister, Sheri, came around ten and visited for two hours with me and Sampson. Mom and Dad came in around 11:30 a.m., and then they took me to lunch at Panera Bread. My friends, Terri Carraway and Shelia Hall, came around 6:30 p.m. before evening visiting hours, and Sampson's nurse made an exception and allowed them to visit. We cackled and laughed, shared stories and had some birthday cake they brought me from Tiffany's Bakery in Columbia, South Carolina. Mom and Dad brought a cake too! We shared both cakes with everyone on 4 West. Sampson's favorite nurse, Brenda, bought a card, helped Sampson sign it, and then bought a singing birthday balloon and had every floor nurse come in to sing and dance for me. I cried. I was touched by all who had poured forth their love for me on my special day. God Bless them all. Sampson's blood pressure was low today, which made him light-headed when standing. This set us back a day for release. It scared him. He is very weak physically, but holding on emotionally. P.S. I can't believe I am feeling this way, but I am fighting some jealously feelings when it comes to Brenda, Sampson's favorite nurse. Deep down I know she has done an awesome job in caring for Sampson and making him as comfortable as possible. But I sense something more or is there a little insecurity on my part that is seeping out? What is wrong with this picture? I am so ready to get home and start living. Just me and Sampson. I need a sense of normalcy. Help me Lord!

*****

Friday, September 28 … Day 18

Sampson was bound and determined to get up and walk today. Dennis (the physical therapist) came in and taught Sampson how to overcome dizziness by looking out and forward, (not down) and reminded him to remember to breathe when he felt dizzy. He moved his bowels and used the bathroom on his own. Not a big deal for most of us, but after what he's been through, these are great accomplishments. Sampson ultimately made three trips around 4 West. Sampson was ready to come home after one lap around, and I said "No!" Because the first trip home just two days after his accident went so wrong I was honestly scared to take Sampson home. From that experience I have learned to trust my instincts. I want to see Sampson with some strength and able to get up on his own, use the bathroom on his own, and not be wanting morphine every two hours. Am I being selfish?

Lori Kay came to stay the night, and we went out to dinner at Macaroni Grill. I pigged out and really overdid it. I think I was releasing a little stress through my fork. Then, when we went back to visit Sampson for the evening, I did my best to keep my frustrations in check. I pretty much always speak my mind with Sampson and holding back on how I really felt about the morphine usage was difficult for me. I was having a hard time putting myself in his place. I knew he had been through a lot and I knew the hospital's philosophy was "whatever it takes so that our burn patients feel no pain" yet I knew we would *be on our way home in just a matter of days, and then what? What's wrong with me? Why am I being so difficult?! Help me Lord!*

I love my husband!

*****

The next morning, Lee Ann came in and we had breakfast together. During breakfast she asked me how I slept.

"I didn't sleep all that well," I said. "All I could think about was spiders."

"Me too," she said. We'd both had enough spiders to last us a while.

After breakfast I called Sampson Jr. on his cell phone, just checking in with him to see what was going on. While we were talking, he said, "Be careful what you say. I've got you on speakerphone," and laughed.

That sounded a little odd. "Where are you? Why am I on speakerphone? Who else is there?"

As it turns out, he *did* have me on speakerphone. And there was somebody else there alright. There were a lot of "somebodys" there because he was at the farm with probably twenty-five or thirty other people.

They had all gone to the farm to pick the rest of the corn.

It was all I could do to hold back the tears.

Everybody was standing around Sampson Jr., and while he had them on speakerphone, he told me what they were going to do. At first I was too stunned to say much more than a strained "Thank you ... and be safe."

I thought to myself, how in the world did all these guys end up at my farm to harvest the corn? Someone had to have organized this.

A lot of people from work came down and several people from around the area brought their corn pickers. I think all together they had four or five tractors with corn pickers at the farm ready to go.

By the end of the day they had picked all twenty-five acres of corn, bagged it, and stacked it in the barn. I just couldn't believe it. Once I was out of the hospital, I made a point to thank everyone who was there that day.

Up to this point, I had never done anything like what they had done. I'd never really gone out of my way to help someone. What they did that day made a real impression on me. The thing is, a lot of people never take the time to do things for other people. I know because I was the same way.

And again, it's not that I didn't want to. Not at all. I'd like to think that if I had really known about somebody who needed my help, I would have given it in a minute. It's just that, like so many people today, I was always busy working at my job, being with my family, or spending time out on the farm. But seeing something like that … all those people out there because of me … it changes you. That was really special. And because of everything that happened in those months, capped off by such a demonstration of unselfish love by that group of people at the farm, I've started doing a lot more for other folks. Maybe one day we'll all take the time to do things like that for other people.

My friends Terri and Tim Caraway brought a camera and a camcorder with them. They took a lot of pictures and filmed the whole day. Then another friend, Lisa Phelps, took the still photographs and put them to music.

About two months later, Lee Ann and I saw the video for the first time and cried like babies through the whole thing. In the past, I had never shown much emotion. But that was starting to change. My emotions were raw and starting to evolve.

One man brought his two young sons with him to the farm that morning. While the boys were playing in the corn field, they found the pocket knife I had used to cut off my arm. The amazing thing was, they found it lying pretty far away from the burned corn picker. And it was still covered with blood.

As best I can figure, it must have been thrown there when the tire exploded. The boys gave the knife to Sampson Jr., and he decided to keep it until the next time he saw me. For Christmas that year, Heather Johnson bought a shadow box to put it in. To this day the knife is displayed in that shadow box on the kitchen wall in our home. It is a daily reminder of God's grace.

That evening, we were still talking about what a wonderful thing had happened out at the farm when my doctor came in and made the day even better.

He told me I could go home the next day. Lee Ann and I were so excited. After three weeks and six surgeries, we were finally going home.

I left the hospital on a bright Sunday morning, one of the finest mornings I could remember in a long time. As Lee Ann and I drove home, I was just happy to be alive and grateful to be able to spend another day with her. If I had ever doubted that God had blessed me with an amazing wife (and I never have), everything we had been through since September 11 was proof of just how strong and loving she is. During the ride, I thanked God for her and for reminding me how blessed I am. I thought about that a lot. And about the people who have played such an important part in my life.

*****

My father was the hardest worker I have ever known. I guess he had to work hard to provide for a wife and seven children. And my mother made sure our home was kept clean, our clothes were washed, and that we had hot meals on the table three times a day. She also made sure all the children were in Sunday school and church every Sunday. As for the rest of my family, all of my sisters and brothers graduated from high school and several went on to finish college degrees, while others served in the armed forces.

My basketball coaches, Harold Combs and Glen Peace, instilled in me the drive to never give up, to never quit. To do whatever it takes to be a winner. This is part of what gave me the fortitude to do what it took to not give up on my life while I was stuck in that corn picker.

My life really began to change when Avery Howard hired me and gave me the chance to learn how to operate a roller on the night shift with Blythe Industries (Now Blythe Construction, Inc.). Later in my career he taught me the importance of planning, managing, and looking at the big picture when it came to the job. To this day I still use a lot of what he taught me in my work.

After finishing the project in Middlesboro, Kentucky, the superintendent I was working for at that time, Ken Hensley, asked me if I wanted to go to Greenville, South Carolina. Blythe had a dam project under construction, and they needed some additional workers. Ken told me I would have to take a cut in pay from $7 per hour to $6 per hour, so I had to really think about that over the weekend. But, with no work in Kentucky for an inexperienced 19-year-old and Ken giving me an opportunity to operate equipment, I decided to go for it. The dam project was tough on me. I had never been away from home, so I was in a strange place. Ken took me under his wing and not only taught me how to run equipment, but also kept me busy during my off time. He had a farm in the mountains, so on the weekends that I didn't go home, I would help him on his farm. When it came to work, at the farm or on the job, Ken was a go-getter. He thrived on beating deadlines. That attitude is now a part of my working style thanks to Ken's influence.

When we finished the dam project, the next job was in Columbia, South Carolina building a portion of I-20 and the I-77 interchange. At this point I was a finish dozer operator and was back to making $7 per hour. I had just bought a new F150 Ford pickup and was having a blast at the age of 21. However, I did have a dream. I wanted a company truck and my own farm one day. I would sit on my dozer and watch Ken drive by, and would start thinking about how I wanted to be just like him.

In addition to farming, Ken also liked to dance, so on the weekends he would go to a shag club called Studebaker's. The shag is a southern dance. I learned that it started on the strands between Myrtle Beach, South Carolina, and Wilmington, North Carolina, during the 1940s, and is really popular among the beach music crowd. I had always been around country and bluegrass music, so this was different from anything I had ever experienced in Kentucky. Beach music and dancing was sure different — not really my thing.

Even so, I'd go with him to Studebaker's just to have something to do. Like I said, it wasn't really my thing, but sometimes Ken wouldn't go unless somebody else went. So I'd go down there with him, hang out, and watch folks dance since I'm not a dancer myself.

One of the last times I was there, a woman came up and asked me to dance with her. "No thank you," I said. "I appreciate the offer, but I can't dance." I was trying to be cool about it, but the fact is, it kind of scared me. I wasn't use to women walking up and asking me to dance.

She turned around, put her head down, and headed back to her table. Then I felt bad because I thought I had hurt her feelings.

"Wait a minute," I said. "I mean, I can't dance to this shag music, but when they play the next slow song I'd be happy to slow dance with you." She said, "OK, that will be great," and headed back to the group of women at her table.

About thirty minutes later, a slow song came up, and before I knew it, she was standing right there beside me. So we slow danced and talked. Little did I know that dance would change my life, because the girl I met was Lee Ann. One of the girls she worked with was having a birthday, so she came with a group from work for the party.

We dated steadily for a few months. Once the Columbia job was finished, I was moved to Asheville, North Carolina. It was a small job that only took a couple of months to complete. Then my next job was in Charlotte, North Carolina. But the difference was, instead of going to Kentucky on the weekends, now I was going to Lugoff to see Lee Ann.

At 22, I made grade foreman with the company while we were building a golf course. And I was still going back and forth between work and Lee Ann. We dated the whole time I was moving around. When I heard the company had picked up another job in Columbia, I volunteered to go.

Talk about a man who had it all. I didn't see how life could get much better. As a grade foreman I had a company truck and was moving up in the company. And I had a steady girl. I remember thinking more than once, "Man, this is great."

After living in a hotel for a couple of months and continuing to see Lee Ann, I thought, "I just need to marry her." After all, by that point we had been dating about two years, and we were both thinking along the same lines.

By now I was back with Avery Howard, the superintendent who originally hired me. One afternoon I went to him and said, "Avery, I need to take Friday afternoon off." I was one of those guys who never missed work, so I was pretty sure he wouldn't have a problem with it. So when I asked him, he said, "Sure. No problem. But what do you want to be off for?"

I told him I had to go do some paperwork.

"Are you buying a truck or something?"

"No," I said. "I'm going to get a marriage license."

His eyes got really big and he said, "What? You're getting married?

Really?" I think he was about as excited as I was. "Sure. Take off whatever time you need to."

The next week I went back to him and said, "Avery, I need to be off again this Friday afternoon."

He looked at me with a kind of funny expression on his face. "Why? What are you doing now?"

"Friday we're going over to the courthouse in Camden to get married." I'm sure he thought that was pretty strange, but Lee Ann had been married once before and she didn't care anything about having a second church wedding, and that was fine with me. The important thing to me was that I was going to marry the woman I loved. Plus, we really didn't want a big wedding; we both agreed that there were more practical things we could spend our money on. Lee Ann was a teller at SAFE Federal Credit Union and had just been promoted to head teller. With the new position she got a little raise. Although she wasn't making a lot of money she lived modestly and had been able to put some aside. Lee Ann was a single mom and knew she needed to provide for her two children. She had just bought a modest starter home. As such, there were a number of improvements we wanted to make in order to make it our home.

So, in keeping with our plan, instead of spending a lot on flowers, dresses, tuxedoes, and all the extras, we were going to the courthouse where Lee Ann's children, Tiffany and Luke, would be our witnesses.

Interestingly enough, Lee Ann had never met my parents, so a couple of days before the wedding I called them and told them I was getting married. Then, after the ceremony, we drove to Kentucky, and she finally met my mom and dad.

And from that day, I've never looked back.

*****

The first thing I saw when we got home was a big yellow sign with black letters that said "Welcome Home Sampson." One of the neighbors had made it and I remember thinking, "That's so cool."

For the next two weeks different neighbors brought us dinner every night. After all the hospital food, I was really thankful for all that good home cooking. As the days passed, I started to get my strength back and began gaining some weight. But every day still brought new challenges. It was hard to do almost anything. The fingers on my left hand were still taped up, and my right leg was in a splint to keep me from bending my knee so the skin graft would heal. And the worst part of all of this was when Lee Ann had to clean me up after I used the bathroom. But there was no other way because of all the constraints I was faced with. Still, it was awkward, embarrassing, and I felt so helpless.

*****

Saturday, September 29 … Day 19

I drove Sampson home from the Augusta Burn Center today. I was excited and scared at the same time. I was so ready to get home and yet I wondered if I was going to be able to care for him the way the nurses had. Why am I second guessing myself? We left at 1 p.m. and arrived home around 4 p.m. The ride home was wonderful. It was a beautiful fall day. The colors seemed brighter than ever, and everything was crisp and clear. It's like all outdoors was happy! I can't begin to explain the overwhelming feelings of thankfulness to God who is allowing me this time with my husband. I feel as though I am on the top of the world and can conquer anything that comes my way!

Sampson Jr. was at the house to greet us, and the neighbors had placed a "Welcome Home Sampson" banner that was stretched across the two columns as you walk up to the front door and there were balloons everywhere.

Lori Kay was instrumental in helping me get organized for the trip home. She took care of getting all the prescriptions filled and running some errands for me at Target. What would I do without her? She is a Godsend for sure. Sampson was really alert and in tune with everything that was going on.

Our first day at home was simple. The only guests were Lori Kay and Heather. For dinner it seemed fitting that we had our all-time favorite meal, chicken wings! Back to normal?

*****

Sunday, September 30 … Day 20

Today was the first day Sampson didn't need to take a nap. His strength must be returning. Lori Kay, Sampson Jr., Heather, and I went to church today and then were treated to a great Sunday lunch prepared by our neighbors Elaine and Roy Schmiedeshoff. Being in church stirred a lot of emotions. During these last few weeks I have been closer to God than ever. Being in church was a blessing and I rightly gave thanks to God. Steve, Colt, and Delia came over and joined us for lunch.

After lunch we spent some time with Sampson, and then the family went to work. We washed the dog, trimmed the stray sprouts off the Crepe Myrtle trees, got rid of the outdoor potted plants that had died due to the absence of my watering, swept the garage, and put the filing cabinet together that I had ordered prior to Sampson's accident and had been delivered while we were in Augusta. Then we gathered up all the garbage for Steve to take off to the landfill. I know people talk about Sunday being a day of rest, but the Bible also talks about not leaving your ox in the ditch, and today was definitely an ox in the ditch day. But it was also a good, productive day. Things were beginning to take shape; we were starting to feel a little more "normal."

In the meantime, we had a few more visitors and Sampson slept well that night.

*****

Monday, October 1 ... Day 21

Today was busy. First, I went grocery shopping, and by the time I got home and put everything away, half the day was gone. Then I started the process of trying to get our lives back to some semblance of order.

Sampson's biggest concern today was his bowels. They hadn't moved since Thursday, and he was becoming uncomfortable. He wanted to call the doctors in Augusta. No, scratch that. He wanted me to call them. But I felt this was something he could do himself. We went back and forth. Nothing new there. I finally gave in and called because I didn't have the energy to play the game. I got through and the nurse who answered said the doctor would get back to us in the afternoon. Sampson asked me to go to drugstore and talk to the pharmacist.

I came home with magnesium citrate, suppositories, and more stool softeners. We followed all the various instructions to the letter and ... nothing. By now Sampson had begun to fret and worry to the point that it was getting on my nerves. By late in the evening, I even said something mean like, "I'll be sure to write the wimp chapter in your book."

When we finally heard back from the doctor, he said the one sure way to move the bowels was an enema. That wasn't exactly the news he wanted to hear.

It was an exhausting day emotionally and physically. I can't believe it was only our third day home from the hospital and I was already experiencing anger and frustration. What is up with this? Why am I feeling this way? I need your help Lord. I can't do this on my own.

*****

Tuesday, October 2 … Day 22

Sampson woke with a positive attitude, and right after breakfast we went to work. We followed the doctor's advice from the day before and hoped for the best. After an hour of waiting we were about to pull out the map and make another trip to the hospital when … success! You would have thought Santa had come. Sampson said he was so relieved that he felt like a new man. For the next hour I worked on getting him cleaned up, including shaving off his beard, washing his hair, and getting him a bath. He was even starting to look like a new man, or at least the Sampson I remembered.

I spent most of the day cleaning and washing clothes, making lunch, and tending to Sampson's needs. We had several visitors today. Sue, our neighbor from down the street, brought us a beautiful fruit basket. Two of the equipment managers from Blythe Construction, Inc., Steve Burleson and Jason Mooney, came with a beautiful basket full of chocolates and Get Well cards. Preacher Gene also came by at Sampson's request and spent a couple of hours with us. Sampson wanted to talk to him about baptism. And one of the main topics of conversation was God's grace and how it was obvious that God was there with Sampson. Any one of a number of things could have cost Sampson his life, but God's hand was evident in everything that happened: (1) Sampson never passed out during his ordeal, even with all the blood he lost. (2) The tire explosion that blew him away from the fire happened at exactly the right time. (3) After everything else that happened, Sampson was able to drive his truck to the road. (4) Doug Spinks was the first person who stopped. The fact that he was even on that road at that time was a miracle.

We talked about loss and how our body can't distinguish between types of loss. To the mind, loss is a loss. Preacher Gene said that Sampson would probably go through many of the stages of loss, including anger and depression. He gave us a lot to think about. It was awesome to see my husband so engaged with Preacher Gene and knowing that he was taking the steps to commit his life to God. Even though it took something as horrific as Sampson's accident to get to this point I was so overjoyed! On the other hand hearing Preacher Gene speak to the possible emotional roller coaster that may be ahead of us was scary. Am I ready for this, emotionally, physically, and spiritually? I was having some doubts. Once again I asked God to help me, help him, to get through all of this.

*****

Over the next few weeks, a lot of friends and family come to visit me, and I am convinced that their outpouring love and support were a significant part of my healing process.

My boss, Brian Webb, brought me my phone and computer from work and came by several more times just to visit. He kept me updated on what was going on at the job site.

The guys from work brought me a huge basket full of chocolates and get well cards including this huge get well card that had been signed by many of my coworkers. A lot of them even wrote personal messages. Judy Sellers, the human resource director from work, had been so busy taking phone calls about me that she wrote that she felt like she had become my personal secretary. Many of the people who had worked for Blythe Construction, Inc. throughout the years were calling Judy to see how I was doing, and she made a list of everyone who had called. Later I made sure to return their calls and thank them for their support and prayers.

Subcontractors who had worked on projects with me also called with their support and prayers. One in particular gave me very generous monetary gift, which was a great help with our mounting expenses. And while we had known each other for years, I couldn't believe the outpouring of love and support from him and so many other people. People I didn't even know were calling to tell us they were praying for my family and me.

Our son Luke had married his wife, Faith, three months earlier. Faith's mother and step-father, Carole and Matt Halley, and Faith's grandmother Margaret Nelson who had only known us a couple of months, sent significant monetary gifts. It was hard to comprehend their generosity. We were strangers to them, yet they opened their hearts and provided for us at a time when there were numerous expenses. These and all the other things so many people did for us taught us some important lessons about loving others; important lesson we continue to remember and practice ourselves.

The President (at the time), Bill Capehart and Vice President (now serving as president), Alan Cahill of Blythe Construction, Inc. also came to see me. I told them I was eager to get back to work and would not be out much longer. They both encouraged me to take as much time as I needed to get back to work. I told them I planned to be back at work by Thanksgiving, but they encouraged me not to hurry back until I had healed sufficiently.

I was not expecting that kind of news, and I don't mind telling you it was a huge relief. I had worked for Blythe for twenty-five years, but I have a feeling that it wouldn't have mattered how long I had been with the company. Bill and Alan would have made that same visit to any employee in a similar situation and delivered the same news. They are both great people. Two of the best leaders Blythe has ever had.

The other big surprise of the day came when the equipment managers from work, Steve Burleson and Jason Moony, brought my company truck back to me. They did a great job getting all the blood out of the truck, even though there was so much on the front seat that they finally just had to replace it. But they also fixed the door from where I hit the tractor after the accident. I had forgotten I had done that until Sampson Jr. reminded me about it while I was still in the hospital. The day after the accident while in ICU, I remembered that I had left the truck in the road, and asked Sampson Jr. to go move it.

"Paps," he said after he got back, "I don't see how in the world you survived. I've never seen so much blood in one place in my life. And the door was bent all the way up until it touched the front quarter panel of the truck. How in the world did you manage to do that?"

At first I didn't remember. Then, it all came rushing back.

"For some reason when I got in the truck I put it in reverse, and I had the passenger's door open," I said. "I was in a hurry to get out of there, and I hit the tractor with the door before I thought to put the truck in drive."

"Well you hit it a good one," he said.

Later that morning Jennie Rector from LPA Engineering, one of the design build engineers, came by to see me. She brought a big cooler full of great gifts from her group. The cooler was full of books, magazines, candy, and even pumpkin ale for Halloween, which was right around the corner. We were talking about our two new design build projects when my brother, Steve, stopped in to see me.

We thanked Steve for helping us and for being there for us, but sometimes "thank you" just doesn't seem like enough. And I know we're family and that's the kind of thing family does for each other, but even so, he had taken a lot of time off of work to help us. Things would have been harder to manage without his help, and I'll always be grateful.

*****

Wednesday, October 3 … Day 23

Pain and nerve activity continue to haunt Sampson and yet he continues to become more independent and more relaxed with his donor site and right arm. He is now brushing his own teeth. In the mornings and evenings, he opens and closes the shades. He can use the bathroom by himself, and he has begun to sleep and rest on his left side. I know these seem like small accomplishments but, they are so helpful and mean so much to me. My parents reared me to be an independent person, but it takes a lot out of me when I have to do everything on my own. I hate that Sampson has to deal with the pain that those bundled up nerves in what's left of his right arm are causing!

He had two visitors and took two naps.

We had a cleaning service come in for four hours today. I needed some help to get the house in order. I hope to be able keep it up from here myself, but it takes a lot of time to tend to Sampson's needs. And I can't say enough about our wonderful neighbors. The neighbors continue to feed us each night. Emily Carter fixed a roast, potatoes, and green beans and Sampson ate two helpings. It was all so good. After that, I ran for the first time in three weeks.

At first I left with the goal of walking two miles. Once I got out there I thought, "It's only been three weeks; surely I can still run". So I did, and it felt great. I was a little winded at the end, but all in all, it was not bad. I continue to struggle with my weight. I must start exercising every day. I need to do this for me. Why can't I be the kind of person who loses weight when under stressful situations?

When I came in, Sampson was on the couch. It didn't take long to realize he was feeling frisky. I thought to myself, no way! First of all, what if I move wrong and hurt his arm or leg? Secondly, should he be doing this? But you know what, I knew he needed this and I was willing to do whatever it took. Making love is like medicine to Sampson. So he got a little dose! What an awesome feeling to be loved again by my man.

One step closer to normal. Or at least, our new normal.

Later that day I talked with Luke and Faith. They are coming to see us in a couple of weeks. Life is good, and God is always good!

Thank you for my husband, friends, and family.

*****

Thursday, October 4 … Day 24

Today was another great day for Sampson. Visitors kept his spirits high and kept him occupied which was a nice break for me. Brian Webb has been a true friend for Sampson. He's been the one person, other than his brother, who has been by his side the entire time. It is so important for Sampson to stay connected to work, and this is where Brian comes in. The pastor at Rocky River Presbyterian Church, Kyle Hite, came by today and visited for a couple of hours. While Sampson was humbled and hungry to know Christ I felt it was important for him to get acquainted with Kyle. The church is so close to us, and it's a church where I feel comfortable. I just hope that Sampson and Sampson Jr. will join me for years of worship and service to God through the community. I've heard people say, "Watch what you pray for," but I never imagined that it would take something like this to get my husband churched! If I weren't as strong as I am, I would take this and turn it into a guilt thing. Love you, God!

*****

Friday, October 5 … Day 25

I was "cut loose" for several hours today, so I used the time to do some things I needed to do. I must say that I really needed this time away from Sampson. I needed to do some things for me for a change. I know that if I don't take care of myself I won't be able to take care of Sampson. This was becoming a new rule of survival for me. I went and picked up my new office chair, stopped by LA Weight Loss, and then had my hair trimmed and colored. Before Sampson's accident I was well on my way to losing some pounds I had let creep on me. I have put several back on and it is time for me to get serious or else I will be back at the same weight in no time at all. I hate being overweight. I want to be attractive for Sampson and I always feel better when I am at a healthier weight. This is such a struggle for me. I am definitely a stress eater. Lord I need your help with this. While I was out, I stopped by the grocery store and picked up a few items. It was nice to get away.

While I was gone Sampson had more visitors. Jeannie from LPA Engineering came by and spent a good bit of time with Sampson. They have worked together several years on I-85 jobs, and I can tell there is a lot of respect that flows both ways. She brought a cooler filled with gifts. By far the most anyone has done. It was filled with movies, books, snacks, cheeses, and other things. I know Sampson enjoyed her visit. Then Steve came by and stayed with him until I got home. He sure does love his brother.

Steve is going to the farm with Sampson Jr. tomorrow to plant food plots for the deer. Steve's son, Colt, is going with them. Sampson's bosses came by today for an hour. They made it clear that he was not to rush back to work. I think they comforted Sampson. Jennie Bloodsworth, our neighbor from across the street, came over this evening and stayed a long while. I told Sampson it's amazing how much you learn about each other when you just sit still and take a little time to talk.

I thank God for my time with Sampson.

*****

Saturday, October 6 … Day 26

Sampson Jr. left early this morning to go work on the farm. He planted oats for the deer and carried more corn to Kershaw. He worked really hard. Steve, Colt, and Junior's friend, Kyle Laney, joined him.

The Carraways came and spent several hours with us this evening. Terri brought CDs with pictures and video of the massive corn picking efforts from a couple of Saturdays ago. The pictures were awesome.

We ate chicken wings, laughed, and caught up with them about all the previous events and happenings. By the end of the night, Sampson was pooped from all the visiting, noise, and hot, spicy food. All that, coupled with a late bedtime, set his right arm into action. The nerve endings have gone crazy. He took a lot of medication in order to sleep. Maybe he did too much, too soon. Even so, it is wonderful to be home with my husband, family, and friends. I am so relieved that we are getting back into a routine.

*****

The next day our pastor, Dr. Eugen Rollins, at Liberty Hill Presbyterian Church in Liberty Hill, South Carolina came to see me because I told him I had some things I needed to talk to him about. Dr. Rollins is a true man of God, and he is someone I look up to. He is a gentle man, quick to laugh, and always willing to listen. As we sat in the living room, I told him about the accident. I told him that when I was exhausted and knew I could not possibly free myself, I prayed to God. As I told him about the miracle of how God rescued me, it became obvious to all of us that there were just too many things that happened at "just the right time and in just the right way" for any of this to be a coincidence. Things like me breaking the bone in my arm a split second before the tire exploded, or how he put the right people in the right place to help me (like Doug Spinks and Karen Baker). I told him it was only by the grace of God that I was sitting there talking to him that day.

"I believe that, Sampson," he said. "God has been active throughout history, and His grace is evident in so many ways. And while some people might call what happened to you a miracle, I think you're right. It was more an act of God's grace."

We talked some about my Christian journey, and I shared how I hadn't been baptized as a child and thought it may have had something to do with being scared to death of being taken under water and walking down the aisle in front of everyone. In my heart and mind I was ready many times, but my feet wouldn't take me to the altar. It was so strange because all my brothers and sisters were baptized in my mom's church. My dad didn't go to church when I was growing up, but later professed his faith when he had a close call and almost died. He was baptized and started attending church in his early seventies. So even though I was never formally baptized, I had confessed my sins and had asked Jesus into my life when I was in my early teens.

I told Dr. Rollins that each and every day I remember that it is God who made it possible for me to be here. It is God who has given me the strength and attitude to wake up every day with a thankful heart and the ability to go about every task with a positive attitude. I know He is here for me.

"That's the beauty of grace," Dr. Rollins said. "You can't earn it, and it's not based on what you do. Grace is God's blessing and unmerited favor."

I began to think about that.

Gene had preached a summer series on grace titled *Grace is Not a Blue-Eyed Blonde*, and later published a book based on the sermon series. Before he left, he said he would send me the sermon tapes.

Then I asked him something that surprised even me.

I asked him if he would baptize me when I was able to go back to church.

*****

Sunday, October 7 … Day 27

Today was another day filled with visitors and food. Mom and Dad came up around 10:45 a.m. and sat with Sampson while Sampson Jr., Heather, and I went to church. When we got back, we ate egg salad that I had prepared on the front porch this morning while drinking coffee with Sampson. It was a beautiful morning and it felt like old times to sit and enjoy one of God's greatest gifts — nature. Mom brought the nurse a gift. Yes, that's me. It was an antique plate, rectangle in shape, a light yellow color, with flower appliqués. It was so sweet of her to think of me. She also brought dinner: a taco/enchilada casserole, cheese dip, and guacamole salad. It was delicious and much appreciated. Steve, Delia, and Colt were here and shared the meal. Steve and Sampson sat all afternoon and watched football and then a NASCAR race while Delia and I cleaned Sampson's Ford F150 truck, inside and out. We are taking it to Augusta tomorrow. Sampson Jr. has been driving it back and forth to the farm and it was filthy. I am glad I had some help; otherwise, it would have taken me forever. It was a good day.

CHAPTER 7

The next day Lee Ann and I were back at the Burn Center in Augusta to see my doctor, Dr. Abu Zaheed Hassan, and if everything looked okay, to have the staples removed from my arm. Dr. Hassan came in, checked me over, and said everything looked great. He was pleased with the way my arm was healing.

As he left he smiled and said, "See you next time," then told the nurse to go ahead and remove the staples.

To say having those staples removed was painful is an understatement.

Since my accident no one had ever handled my arm so roughly. Or at least that I could remember, being that this was the first time anybody had worked on it while I was awake … and man, it was painful. As each staple came out, I kept hoping it was the last one. The nerves in my right arm were going crazy, and the nurse could tell I was in a lot of pain. Just like with the infection, it felt like there were worms crawling around inside my arm. I was in so much pain that by the time she finished I was facing the wall with my head buried in a pillow. She knew I was hurting, so she left the few remaining staples in because they were so deep. She started to remove the thin layer of gauze-type material that covered the graft on my right leg, but I'd had enough. I told her I could do that at home. After thinking about it for a moment, she agreed and gave Lee Ann instructions on how to go about the process.

*****

Monday, October 8 … Day 28

Up at 4:30 a.m. and ready to start the day. We left at 5:30 a.m. for Augusta at a nice pace, and after a stop for breakfast we arrived at Doctors Hospital at 8:30 a.m. Sampson insisted on walking in from the parking lot. We went directly to 4 West and said our hellos. The clinic waiting room was warm, stuffy, and extremely small. By 9:15 a.m., it was packed wall-to-wall with young, middle-aged, and older victims of burns and accidents. This was our first visit to the clinic. It was totally different than the privacy of 4 West. The room smelled of healing flesh and old bandages. Sampson was on edge and very uncomfortable. I sensed he didn't want to be there. Around 10:30 a.m. we were called back. The clinic nurse that worked with us had little in the way of bedside manner, but ended up doing a great job at getting Sampson in the right frame of mind. With thirty or more staples removed from his arm, and his wounds cleaned and wrapped, she gave him some pain medication and sent us on our way. It was extremely difficult to be in the room with Sampson while having the staples removed. First because I hated to see him in such pain and second I was getting irritated at his wimpy ways! Here is this huge manly guy who a few weeks earlier cut his own arm off so not to burn to death and yet he was acting like the biggest wimp ever! He laid there on the table with his knees to his chest facing the wall and cried out with every stich removal. Could it have really hurt that bad? Okay, so what happened to my loving caring nursing attitude? It is me again Lord. Help me to be nice and show my husband the love and care he needs. By 3:30 p.m. we were home. Sampson slept most of the way. I was exhausted. When we got home we enjoyed a movie together, ate leftovers and had an uneventful evening. Just what we needed. Good day. Great God!

*****

The next morning I felt like a million dollars. It is amazing what a good night's rest will do for the body and the soul. I was full of energy and started busying myself around the house knowing in the back of my mind there was a major task I needed to accomplish today. No sense in putting it off any longer. I got into our whirlpool tub and after soaking for a couple of hours the water was pretty nasty looking. It had turned red from all the dried blood that had incrusted the gauze to my leg. Eventually the material started to peel away from the new tender skin underneath. Once again, a painful process, but it was nothing like the pain from getting the staples removed from my arm. I was glad I could do this on my own, at my own pace.

*****

Tuesday, October 9 … Day 29

Sampson awoke today feeling better than any other day. He slept through the night and awoke with no pain. He was chipper and ready to do chores.

After breakfast he helped me around the house. He took out the garbage and decided he was tired of seeing the cooler of gifts sitting in the living room. He cleaned out the cooler and organized the snacks that had been given to us by various friends and neighbors. Knowing we had a major chore ahead of us, I convinced him we needed to get started.

Our chore today was to work on removing the cloth that the doctors placed over the donor site when they grafted the skin from Sampson's leg. In the healing process the skin had adhered to the cloth and was stuck to the donor site, his left hand, and three of his fingers. The nurse shared with us the day before that we should have been instructed to remove the cloth before the healing process began. The nurse wanted to remove it for Sampson but, he declined and promised to do it himself the next day. After two bath soakings of thirty to forty minutes each, about half of the job was accomplished. Sampson didn't want me to help. I think he was afraid I would hurt him. He insisted on doing this himself. I felt so helpless. All I could do was pray for him. He did a good job. This wasn't an easy process and I could tell it was painful. The rest of the day, he was in pain and very uncomfortable. The worst part was the pain at the end of what was left of his right arm. It seems that all the stimulation from removing the cloth on the other burned areas made the nerve endings in his arm go crazy. Sampson remains in good spirits.

*****

Wednesday, October 10 … Day 30

Last night Sampson did not sleep well. He was up many times and very uncomfortable. Even though he may not be able to sleep, he is careful not to wake me. He is so kind. Yesterday we didn't change his arm wound bandages. It took enough out of him just to get the cloth off the leg and his left hand. Just the thought of changing bandages made him very anxious. The change went well. Anything to do with the right arm is uncomfortable for Sampson. It is for me too. Not being use to wounds, it scares me. To wash, touch, and apply the ointment to the wound is frightening. I don't want to hurt Sampson, but I want to make sure I clean his wound well enough to keep the healing process moving forward. Steve came by today and had lunch with Sampson. We asked him to come partly because we were in dire need of having our garbage carried off. I am spoiled because Sampson takes the garbage off every day. Our

89

neighbor Sandi brought brownies and visited in the evening. People have been so generous!

God's people are so good.

*****

Thursday, October 11 … Day 31

It was exactly one month ago today. How time flies. Sampson can't believe how much time he lost while in the hospital — the whole month of September. Sampson slept well and woke in a good frame of mind. We had coffee in the living room and enjoyed the first cool day of fall. We opened windows throughout the house and used no air all day. Sampson and I shared an inspirational reading from Chicken Soup for the Unsinkable Soul, a birthday gift from my friend Shelia Hall. It was fun to sit and read with my husband. He is on chapter 13 of a book my sister, Sheri, gave him. It is a story centered on the biblical story of Joseph: God Meant It For Good. I am so proud and pleased that he is reading. In the 20 years we've been married, he has never read a book and by no means do I say this in a negative manner. My husband is a very intelligent man who has worked his way up to a superintendent with a lot of responsibility. It is just that he never took the time to read before his accident.

Wound cleaning today was okay for me but not for Sampson. It is crazy, but the more anxious he becomes the more those nerves in his right arm cause him a lot of discomfort and then he is a mess all day. Tomorrow we are going to try to change bandages earlier in the day right after medicine. I truly hope this helps. I can't stand to see him like this. I ran today. It was so beautiful, and I really enjoyed getting out. Biggest accomplishment: getting all calls made and forms sent out for insurance claims for dismemberment funds. Sampson is so time-consuming it's hard to get anything done.

*****

Lee Ann and I took a walk today. I had shared with her a week or so ago that I was ready to go back to the farm. At that point I didn't know that many of our family and friends had planned a big homecoming for me at the farm. They had planned it for a Saturday. I was so excited that it couldn't come fast enough. Tomorrow was the big day.

Sampson Parker, standing in front of the ruined corn picker that trapped his right hand and arm

Prior to the accident: this is exactly what Sampson was doing when his hand and arm caught in the machine

The charred remains of the corn picker.

Sampson said he "knew better" but ignored the warnings posted on the machinery.

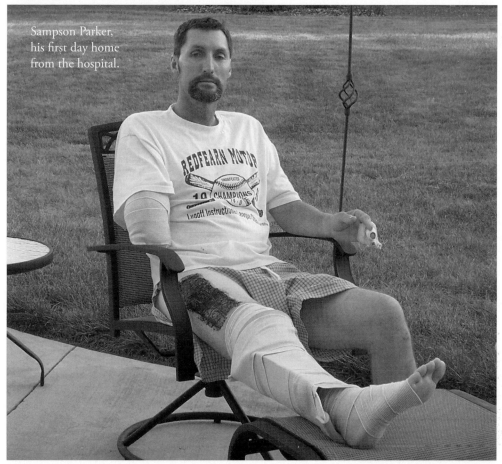

Sampson Parker, his first day home from the hospital.

Sampson harvesting corn
one year after his accident.

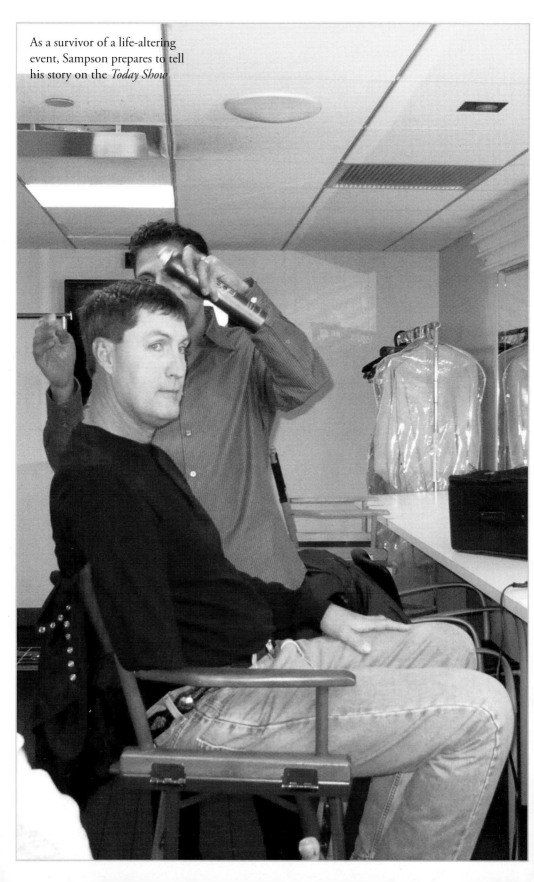

As a survivor of a life-altering event, Sampson prepares to tell his story on the *Today Show*

When we arrived at the farm, there were people everywhere. I didn't think I even knew that many people, but I was glad to see every one of them.

I felt like it was important for me to go back to where it all happened, so the first thing we did was walk down to the corn picker. It was in the same place I almost burned to death just six weeks earlier. I walked around the picker and took a good look at it. On the back of the picker, I saw dried blood all over the sheet metal in the area where I had cut off my arm and had dropped down to break the bone in my arm.

I was fine for a few minutes. After all, I had escaped from this thing and was now celebrating not just that escape, but also the blessing of being surrounded by family and friends. And then it hit me. *Oh God, I almost died right there on that spot … Caught in a machine that did not want to let me go.* It was like the moment in a Stephen King novel where the main character comes back to face the evil person he thought he had once defeated. Except this wasn't a book, and I wasn't a character. And when I understood the full impact of what that place meant, my emotions took over and I started to cry … Hard.

But I didn't want any of my coworkers to see me crying, so I pulled myself together and wiped my eyes. By now some people had spotted me, and they were heading our way. As I looked out into the field, I could see people hand-picking what little bit of corn had been left after the "corn picking party" Sampson Jr. had surprised me with while I was in the hospital. When they saw me they all started to come out from the tall corn stalks, carrying bags of corn.

Most of them were coworkers from Blythe and their family and friends. They had come down from North Carolina to help pick the last of the corn and show their support for me. My friend Joe Turner, one of Blythe's grassing subcontractors, even brought his crew and equipment down from Monroe, North Carolina to plant a cover crop over the picked corn field. They had two tractors running — one plowing and the other one planting winter rye.

Sampson Jr. was using my tractor to plow. He brought the tractor over to me and said, "Hey, do you want to give it a try?"

I wanted to be on that tractor so bad, but I was still very weak. And the last thing I wanted to do was fall off a tractor in front of all those people. So I declined and we all went over to our cabin and picnic shelter instead, where even more family, friends, and coworkers were cooking and setting up for a huge homecoming meal. I was shocked to see so many of my coworkers there. In fact, there were over a hundred people in all.

Doug Spinks was there, and this was the first time I had seen him since my accident. I made a special point to introduce him as the first person who stopped to help me … and the one who saved my life. The crowd gave him a huge, well-deserved round of applause. Then I thanked everyone for coming, and Lee Ann blessed the food. With over a hundred people there, the cooks had prepared an absolute feast. And believe me when I say we put those forks and knives to good use and did our best to make the cooks feel appreciated.

Later my friend and coworker Terry Hensley came over and very quietly handed me an envelope full of money. He said my friends and coworkers wanted to give us this gift as a way to help with whatever we needed.

I tried to say no, but he wouldn't hear of it. We went back and forth a little, but ultimately I didn't want to insult him and the others by refusing such a nice gift. "Terry," I said, "The medical part is pretty well covered. But I'll tell you what. I do need to replace my corn picker. Would that be OK?"

He said that would be great. So I tucked the money away in my pocket, and we headed back to the celebration.

After a couple more hours of visiting with everybody and thanking them for coming, I was exhausted and ready to go back home to Harrisburg.

As I said earlier, the farm is my hobby and road construction is how I make my living. I have been with Blythe for twenty-five years and worked my way up from roller operator to project superintendent while helping to build a lot of roads across the Carolinas. I have met and worked with a lot of good people, but none as good as the group that surrounded me that day.

On the way home, Lee Ann drove while I slept. There wasn't a drop of energy left in me, and this was the longest that I had been outside since my accident. But it was a good kind of exhausted. Lee Ann was tired too, but she had been right beside me all day, like a mother hen watching over her baby chicks. To this day she has never complained about all the things she has had to do for me. She is a true blessing.

Thank you, God, for such a strong woman.

*****

Friday, October 12 … Day 32

We walked outside together for the first time. We walked down Willis, to the left, toward Quail Hollow until we came to the stop sign and went back to the house. We did this twice because on our way back to the house we saw that Emily Carpenter was home and we wanted to return her cake container. It was a beautiful fall morning. The air was crisp and the sky was several shades of blue. No signs of fall color in our area. I felt like a school girl walking down the street with my boyfriend. I was so proud of him and so proud to be his wife. Sampson slept a little more than usual today. He attributed it to the walk. Today brought tears and signs of a little depression. I am thinking that not having much to do and not having the energy to get out and go has made him feel trapped. While sharing how thankful he was to me for all I've done for him, his eyes became teary and he asked for a kiss. I am not worried. These are good signs and good, cleansing tears. It won't be long before we are out of this house. It is very hard to see Sampson cry. It hurts to see him hurt. I just want to cry myself, but I can't and won't. I need to be strong for Sampson. Help me Lord!

Sampson had both morning and evening visitors. Matt Adams from Blythe came mid-morning, and Natalie Lutz and Heather Johnson came in the afternoon. Sampson was delighted to see all of them. He was in less pain today and his right arm was on its good behavior. We waited until late in the evening to clean the wound. It went well.

I love my husband!

*****

Saturday, October 13 … Day 33

Today was Sampson's day. He called it a day out of the jail. We went to the farm for the first time since the accident. The ride down was filled with conversation about who would be there and what Sampson should and shouldn't do or say. He was eager to meet Doug Spinks. The day was brilliant with cool

101

blues and sharp greens. Colors of summer and spring, but yet the coolness of those first spring and fall days remained. No fall colors. Coming down the drive into the farm, we saw a peaceful place humming with people, tractors, and dozens of autos parked in a nice row beside the barn that stretched into the adjacent field. Friends and coworkers from Blythe had gathered to welcome Sampson to the farm by cooking a huge lunch, picking 50 bags of corn, disking, tilling, and planting a cover crop of rye grass for the now picked corn fields. There were people everywhere. It was a sight to behold. Sampson's new picnic shelter was put to good use. We gave Doug Spinks a well-deserved ovation, and I blessed the food and gave thanks and praise to God.

We came home, relaxed, watched the race, and ate wings. Sounds like things are getting back to normal.

Then came the first shocker of a bill.

The phone bill.

$1,063.00

God will provide.

#

Sunday, October 14 ... Day 34

Tired, tired, man. Sampson slept until 9:00 a.m. this morning. Last night's NASCAR race and yesterday's activities just wore him out. I spent time catching up with my journal entries, organizing bills, and reviewing Explanation of Benefits statements. The time alone in my study was refreshing. I didn't mind a bit. When Sampson woke I got dressed and went out for my walk/run. Knowing he wanted me to fix him breakfast I decided to do for me first today. When I got back he had fixed himself some cereal and was busy spending time with Sampson Jr. It was good to see him helping himself. I showered and got ready for church. Sampson Jr. and I went to church and then we all had pizza for lunch. After a bath and wound cleaning Sampson was ready for a field trip. We spent the rest of the afternoon riding around and even took the time to look at new cars. He looked at trucks and I looked at cars. He is so determined to buy new vehicles for me and Sampson Jr.

We had a nice dinner. Heather joined us. No other visitors today. I liked having Sampson to myself. He has vowed to go to church with us next Sunday.

I am looking forward to having my man beside me in church. Thank you God for all you've done for us in our journey of faith while learning to trust in you.

*****

Monday, October 15 … Day 35

We both shed tears today. After our trip to Augusta, GA we watched the "Corn Pick-in" CD Terri Carraway gave us a few weeks ago. Words can't express the feelings we have for our wonderful friends, family, and neighbors. The love and compassion shown by all of those people who went to our farm and harvested our corn for us that day made a huge impact on our lives forever more.

Our trip to GA was safe and uneventful. Praise God! I miss my husband driving. Driving is WORK! I also miss all the piddle time I usually have when we are taking a road trip. I could have written thank-you notes, and a whole bunch of other things. Here I go thinking about myself again. Shame on me!

Sampson has been set free! He is delighted to know that he can walk, exercise, start his own physical therapy, and start getting his life back on track. He did so well today. The remaining staples were removed. His skin graft that didn't take (small parts on the backside of the arm) was removed. His wound was washed and dried. His knee graft is perfect and his donor site is perfect. A physical therapist spent most of the time with us today. She fitted Sampson with a knee compression sleeve and a glove for his left hand. Both of which are part of the healing process for the burns. She also explained the next steps in OT & PT along with giving and demonstrating some exercises Sampson can do now.

We visited 4 West and gave and received lots of hugs. We always feel so blessed when we leave that place. We quickly realized that when we think we are having a tough time all we need to do is look around and we can see that there is always someone else facing difficulties far worse than ours. Thank God for where we are. Your blessings continue to flow … Thank you!

*****

Tuesday, October 16 … Day 36

Another first! Sampson bathed himself today, including washing his hair. Don't get me wrong, I love helping my husband, but woo double hoo! I am so glad he is beginning to do things on his own. One less thing for me to do! He was determined to hang around with me all day. Sampson has decided to try and do without pain pills. Knowing he can't drive while taking pain medication has motivated the separation.

Today was a work day. We went to Lowes and picked up several small items we needed to finish up a few projects. I noticed I seemed a little short. Had we spent too much time together? Were we beginning to get on each other's nerves? I felt Sampson sensed my emotions and was extra careful in how he approached me. We went to Walmart to grocery shop. What a trip. It really wore him out. At the checkout line he asked if I minded if he went to the car. On the way home I made an unusual decision to get fast food. I knew I wouldn't have the energy to cook after putting up groceries and finishing laundry and empting the dishwasher.

Sampson Jr. and his friend Chris Williams were at the house when we got home. Thank you Lord! They carried in the groceries for us. After dinner, Chris's mom, Alice who is an OT came over and did a deep tissue massage on Sampson's hand and showed him some exercises he needed to do to enhance the flexibility of his left hand. He enjoyed her visit. She also brought an unusual device her uncle used when he lost his arm years and years ago. It was a stick shaped like the letter "Y" that he used to assist his missing hand when he farmed. He would tape the stick to his arm and use the "V" portion of the stick to leverage his farm equipment in place of his hand. Now that is what you call an old timey prosthetic device! What an awesome day. More learned, more love, and of course God's grace!

CHAPTER 8

After weeks of recuperating at home and trips back to the Burn Center for checkups and the staple removal, I wanted to get back to work, but my doctor wouldn't release me. It had been over ten weeks since the accident and I was getting cabin fever. I wanted to do something.

Since I couldn't go back to work, maybe I needed a change of scenery. I woke up one morning and said to Lee Ann, "Let's go to the mountains and drive up the Blue Ridge Parkway."

The weekend before my accident, Blythe Construction had a manager's meeting at a beautiful resort called Primland, which just happens to be located in the Blue Ridge Mountains in the Meadows of Dan, Virginia. There were deer everywhere and the streams and waterfalls were beautiful.

While I was there I had the chance to do some fly fishing for the first time, and even though all I caught were a couple of small rainbow trout, I didn't mind. I also got to shoot skeet on a professional course during that trip, but as I remember, I didn't do much better at skeet shooting than I did with the fly fishing. I was shooting with Bill Capehart and Alan Cahill, and they were giving me a hard time about missing so many skeet. Now in my defense, the course was hard, and on that particular day they were both shooting really well. But still, I knew I could do better and told them so. *And the next year following my accident I did. Even with a prosthetic right arm and shooting left handed, I shot better than I had the year before.*

So, armed with my memories from the previous trips to the Blue Ridge, Lee Ann and I left early that morning on our cabin fever adventure. October is one of the best months to drive through the parkway because the leaves are usually at their peak and the fall colors are beautiful. What could be more relaxing than a leisurely drive through a beautiful landscape?

On the way we would be driving right through the job site on I-85, and I told Lee Ann I wanted to stop for just a few minutes to see some of my coworkers and see what they had been doing.

They couldn't believe it when I just showed up.

Matt and Tim, both engineers on the I-85 widening project, were there and they both gave me a big hug. Then they pulled out their phones and started telling the other guys on the job that I was there in the office. Before I knew it, everybody came up to the office to see me. Wow, what an emotional experience. It wasn't easy holding back the tears as they told me the stories of how they had been praying for me. I grinned and told them their prayers had been answered.

As they told me how they heard about my accident that day on the job and that the job came to a complete halt, I was really touched. But because they had heard so many different versions about what had happened, they wanted to hear it from me. I was filled with emotion as I shared my story. Part of the emotion came from the fact that here, face-to-face with them, I felt like I had let my guys down. I mean, here I am — the guy who talks safety day in and day out, and look what I did. What kind of an example had I set?

They were amazed that I had survived, and that led to a lot more questions. I answered them as best I could, and then Lee Ann and I headed back to the truck. I told the guys to be safe and said I hoped to be back at work in couple of weeks.

As we drove off I couldn't wait to get back to work. They had replaced me with another superintendent on the assumption that I was going to be out for a long time. And while I knew that made sense from a business standpoint, it made me even more determined to get back to work. I didn't want someone else to finish the job that I had started two years earlier. This was an 85 million dollar road widening project that would expand the road from four lanes to eight. It involved three miles of roadway and two interchanges, including the complete removal of the old roadway and installation of a new concrete roadway. On top of that we had to keep the I-85 traffic moving the whole time. This was Blythe Construction's second design build project, and I had been selected to be the superintendent on both of them. So I wasn't about to let somebody else finish my job if I was physically able to do it myself.

Lee Ann and I continued to drive toward the parkway, thoughts of finishing what I started were buzzing through my head.

I wanted to drive, but she didn't think it was a good idea right then because of all the traffic. She thought it would be better to wait until we reached the parkway for me to drive. Man, I couldn't wait. I had to prove to her (and to myself) that I could drive with one hand.

Once we were on the parkway, I jumped into the driver's seat and took off. At first it felt sort of strange, but after a few minutes I started to adjust. I could tell Lee Ann was nervous, so I slowed down and drove with a little more caution than usual. Since it was the middle of the week, there weren't many people out taking scenic drives. It was as if we had the whole Blue Ridge Parkway to ourselves.

We stopped at a walking trail to take some pictures and take a walk. I did okay walking down the trail, but when we started back to the truck, the trail was uphill all the way and it just about wore me out. That was the first time I had done any real physical exercise since my accident. But I didn't tell Lee Ann because I wanted to get back to work as soon as possible, and showing how that relatively easy effort (compared to what I could normally do) almost wiped me out would only have put things off even longer. In fact, if Lee Ann had known how bad I really felt, she probably would have turned around and taken me home right then.

We made it back to the truck, and I let her drive this time. We drove for miles through Virginia on the beautiful parkway until we found a little motel. Since we hadn't done much in the way of planning the trip we hadn't made reservations, and we were both glad to find a place to stay without much trouble. We checked in, had dinner, and went to bed exhausted.

The next day we were up early. It was a foggy and rainy morning so we ate breakfast, then decided to go back to North Carolina. The fog was so thick that we could only see twenty or thirty feet in front of us, and driving conditions were hazardous at best. I had never seen fog that thick in my life. And to make it worse, unlike the previous day, we couldn't see any of the beautiful fall colors. Just gray fog and the reflection of our headlights.

Lee Ann was relieved once we were out of the mountains and fog, and so was I. From that point on the drive was much easier, and we were able to relax a little. And despite the fun we'd had the day before, we were both glad to be back at home in Harrisburg.

*****

Wednesday, October 17 … Day 37

Ever since Sampson was released from the hospital, he talked about wanting to take me to the mountains to see the fall leaves. At first I just went along with it because I knew it was important for him to have a goal, even though I wasn't sure it was such a good time to take a road trip. And the last thing we needed to do was blow a couple hundred dollars, with all the hospital bills that were coming in. But by 10:30 a.m., after going back and forth about where to stay and whether or not we needed to make reservations, we were on our way to the Blue Ridge Parkway in Virginia.

We made a stop or two on the way, one at Sampson's job on I-85. The visit was pleasant and short. Sampson got to see some of the guys who weren't able to come to the farm, and everybody was glad (and surprised) to see him out there.

After we left the job site, we stopped at Baker's Shoe Store and picked up Sampson's new Red Wing boots. His only other pair burned in the corn picker, so he needed some new ones. Since we weren't in a big hurry we decided to stop at the entrance of the parkway where there was an antique store, garden shop, and deli. We wandered through the shops, strolled along the street, and even had an ice cream. In the past this most likely wouldn't have happened. Sampson would have been in too much of a hurry. But today we just took our time and enjoyed the time together.

Then we drove along the parkway for several hours just enjoying the views and the quiet. Very few people were there because it was the middle of the week. I was a little disappointed in the colors. They hadn't really begun to peak, which is unusual for that time of year.

We stopped at Mabry Mill to look around. We went into the gift shop and then took a few pictures of the mill. At first I thought Sampson wouldn't want his picture taken, but it didn't faze him a bit. We continued North on the parkway since we arrived a little earlier than expected and had some extra time. We found a pull-off overview area, sat in our truck, and had a snack. We talked about everything that had happened over the past couple of weeks, and once again Sampson shed a few cleansing tears. He asked me why it was that his tears seemed to flow so easily now and that led to a deep and personal conversation unlike any we've ever had before.

We arrived at the motel and took it all in. Our room was just okay. The décor was old; the view was … well, actually, there wasn't one. There wasn't even a porch to sit on to enjoy the outdoors. But it was clean. I originally wanted the coziness of a B&B, but we compromised on a local motel. We had dinner reservations at 7 p.m., so while waiting to be called we enjoyed the evening on a deck that was connected to the restaurant and overlooked the woods. We saw three does nibbling on grass as the sun set. So romantic!

We were finally called in, and it was worth the wait. Dinner was the best. After dinner we retired to our room and enjoyed an evening of intimacy for the second time. Sampson has such a will to move on and enjoy our life together. Thank you, Lord, for my husband. Thank you for the means to enjoy each other's company in ways like this.

*****

Thursday, October 18 … Day 38

The next morning we were awake and ready to go before the sun even came up. Sampson's natural internal clock was back in operation. Knowing you can't see much on the parkway in the dark, I managed to get a little more sleep. After showers and packing, we headed out to fuel up and for breakfast. We ate a yummy country style breakfast at Becky's (they're known for their homemade apple pies, crust and all) and purchased two pies to take home with us.

The rest of the drive was difficult. There was heavy fog and rain most of the way, with only a few spots here and there that were clear enough for us to take in the view. But when we could see, we saw a lot of wildlife. Deer and turkeys mostly. The colors in North Carolina were much fuller than those in Virginia. We just couldn't see enough of them.

We stopped at a trading post and had homemade fudge. That left both of us vowing to get back on track as soon as we got home. Then it was back on the road and more fog. After a few more miles, I couldn't do any more, so we turned around and got off the parkway. It was time to head home. We stopped at Gander Mountain to look at left-handed guns. They were so heavy. I felt sad for Sampson. After so many years of good shooting, now he can barely lift a gun. My heart was heavy and I started to cry, but quickly turned away because I didn't want Sampson to see me. Would my husband ever be able to do the things he loved so much before his accident?

Later I asked him if that got him down. His response was "No way." He had too many things to be thankful for.

God has blessed us richly.

*****

Friday, October 19 … Day 39

The rain came today. It has been so long since it rained that we have forgotten what it sounds like, feels like, and smells like. We sat out on the front porch and watched it rain while we had coffee. Sampson began to make calls. While he was talking to his brother, I left him on the porch. He spent a good deal of time catching up with his brother. After breakfast Sampson bathed himself and was ready to go. We had noticed that the end of his right arm wasn't as round as it had been and that there seemed to be a knot forming on the inside. I knew it had to be unwrapped. The task began, and as usual, Sampson became very anxious.

The special silver healing tape that covered his wound was stuck. We soaked it off. The wound was very pink and raw. The Ace bandage was too tight and had caused some swelling. That was what caused the arm to be less round than it should have been. Sampson looked at the wound for the first time since Monday's visit when they removed the graft areas that didn't take. When he came out of the bathroom, he was furious and unhappy with the overall progress. He was down most of the day.

That was a first.

It was dark, rainy, and dreary, which didn't help because his emotions are highly affected by the weather. But as the day progressed, he began to snap out of his darkness as he recalled the scripture he had read that morning about pity.

We enjoyed a homemade Mexican meal and we watched a couple of movies Heather had brought to us. Thank you, God, for being in Sampson's life.

*****

Saturday, October 20 … Day 40

We called the doctor yesterday because Sampson noticed that he had lost the mobility in his right shoulder and was unable to lift his arm above his head. The doctor said he should stop the physical therapy exercises and see an orthopedic doctor in our area as soon as we could get an appointment.

Sampson and Sampson Jr. left for the farm around 9 a.m. I had the day to myself, so I got busy cleaning the house. Even though we had the people from Maid-In-Heaven cleaning service in on Thursday, there was some additional cleaning that needed to be done. Plus, with the two Sampsons gone, I also had the opportunity to catch up with some paperwork. At 2:30 p.m. I picked up Heather and we made our way down to South Carolina. We weren't in a big hurry, so we stopped at several antique stores and browsed. It was so much fun. After we finished shopping we went into Lugoff, did some grocery shopping, and picked up chicken wings from Leos. It was just like old times. I missed my husband today. In fact, this was the first day we have been separated since the day after the accident. But I didn't worry. I knew he was in good hands with Sampson Jr.

We both had time to do some things we really wanted and needed to do. I got some work done, had a girls' afternoon with Heather, and Sampson spent most of the afternoon personally thanking the local farmers who helped pick his corn.

Thank you, God, for friends and family — your angels!

*****

Sunday, October 21 … Day 41

Less than two months, and Sampson is back on the tractor and sitting beside me in church on Sundays. Who would have imagined? Sampson Jr. and Heather woke early and went deer hunting. Sampson and I enjoyed the morning sipping coffee, talking, and looking out at the pond. We had a big breakfast (the kids cooked the eggs), then we got ready for church and headed to Liberty Hill. It was wonderful to be in church as a family. The members were so excited to see Sampson. Preacher Gene even mentioned him twice during the service.

Sampson was very emotional. Many people, many hugs, and many tears … his tears. He is astounded by the number of times he has teared up and how easy the tears flow. As best as I can, I try to help him understand the new emotions he's feeling and that tears are cleansing and part of the on-going healing process.

The sermon was awesome and perfectly timed. Pastor Gene preached about the turmoil between the cross and material things when it comes to wealth. I still struggle with Sampson's determination to buy Sampson Jr. and me our favorite vehicles. But my husband is an awesome, strong, determined, and focused man. I am amazed at his strength and his ability to get up and go on every day. Today's accomplishments were once again a dose of medicine for him.

Plowing, driving the tractor, and shooting his dad's old 30-30 left-handed. His recovery has been amazing. He says he can now shoot better left-handed than Sampson Jr. can when using his right hand.

God, Your Grace is Endless!

*****

Monday, October 22 ... Day 42

Today Sampson graduated from the tub to the shower. And for his first shower since the accident, he did great. The only area that has not been exposed to water is his right arm, and today was the first day he has been cleared to get it wet. The areas where the skin graft didn't take are very pink and tender. I just knew he would be worried about putting it in the water, but it was no problem and he did wonderfully.

He said today was the cleanest he's been since the day before the accident.

Steve came by and had lunch with us. We hadn't seen him in over a week. He seemed more relaxed and himself. Sampson has been worried about him. The last couple of times he visited he seemed a little down.

Sampson and Sampson Jr. worked together yesterday morning before Sampson Jr. went to school. They cleaned out both trucks and put away hunting stuff. They also took care of car repairs: brakes and oil for mine, and an inspection for Sampson Jr.'s truck. I wrote some thank you notes, created a spreadsheet to keep track of insurance claims and medical bills. I also made calls to the insurance company to make sure we understood our out-of-pocket expense amounts.

I don't know what my problem was today. I was short with Sampson and seemed to get agitated very easily. I'm mad at myself for regaining about six lost pounds, and I'm not able to get back in the groove. Didn't get to do much for myself today, not even a shower. I must not lose focus.

Oh God, help me!

*****

Tuesday, October 23 … Day 43

What a wonderful, productive day. Sampson and I began our day with coffee while he read his book and I wrote in my journal. The three of us had a healthy breakfast together. I stopped cooking those big breakfasts and put Sampson back on cereal and skim milk. He looks healthy and has gained back several pounds. The Sampsons went for haircuts and then to buy gas for the mower. I took the opportunity to get out on my own. I really needed a break.

While I was out, I did something for myself. I went to LA Weight Loss and spoke with my counselor. I have gained seven pounds during this ordeal, and I am starting to hate myself for letting it happen. I have done well this week, avoiding the sweets, but haven't cut down enough on my favorite indulgence. Why couldn't I have been designed more like my sister, Lori Kay, and lose my appetite when stressed? I know what my problem is, I just can't seem to cut down the intake of my very favorite indulgences. I went shopping for Faith's (our son, Luke's wife) birthday gift so I could get it in the mail today. I also went to Walmart to pick up a few items for the cabin and the house.

I am getting frustrated with my hair, so I stopped by and made an appointment for a cut on Friday.

Sampson and I cooked hamburgers on the grill, sat out on the back porch, and then ate by candle light. Sampson did a lot of physical work today, including putting in a new water pump by the dog's kennel and pulled weeds. Sampson Jr. cut the grass, and Sampson blew off the cuttings. He said using the blower was difficult. He had another great shower and was brave as I cleaned his wound.

God, you meet all our needs and we thank you.

*****

Wednesday, October 24 … Day 44

This was a day spent visiting at work, with friends, and with doctors. Sampson was up early reading his book. His shoulder has been giving him a fit, and he just knows it was injured during the accident. The physician we contacted at Doctors Hospital suggested we get a referral to an orthopedic doctor and stop the physical therapy for a while. Once Sampson was checked out, the news came back that he has nothing but a frozen shoulder from holding it in the same protective position for so many weeks. So now it's back to stretching and using his right shoulder as much as possible. We also have an appointment with a hand/arm orthopedic specialist in two weeks.

We stopped by Blythe's main office for several hours. We spoke to everyone from accounting clerks and mechanics to the vice president. It was the first time I had been there in the 20 years we've been married. The people were wonderful to both of us, and they were happy to see him.

We had lunch at Chili's, and then went to visit Tommy Cochran and his wife, Barbara. Tommy is getting older and has had a hard time fighting a number of illnesses. Sampson met Tommy years ago and always admired his hard-work and beautiful cattle farm. Tommy helped Sampson purchase the first cows for the farm in South Carolina. Throughout those first few years of cattle farming, Tommy was Sampson's teacher and friend. For us, the visit was long overdue and they were glad to see us.

Sampson Jr. is about to go crazy trying to find a truck. He dragged his dad to Morrison's Used Autos to see what they had. It was a long day and Sampson is tired, but it has been a good day. God will provide and give us the strength to endure.

*****

Thursday, October 25 … Day 45

Thank God for the glorious rain.

We have had an unusual year weather-wise and have had less rainfall than normal. But boy, we got the rain today. That slow, all-day-long kind of drizzle that soaks the ground. Despite all our efforts before the accident to water the grass so it would stay green, while we were in Augusta it turned crispy brown. But that has turned around, and now the grass is as green as green can be.

Today was a day to catch up on some paperwork and write a few more thank you notes. We have so many people to thank. Sampson and I also drove down to Lancaster, South Carolina to pick up the ambulance run report. That's the incident report from the responding EMS unit on the day of the accident and is part of the paperwork required for the dismemberment insurance claim. We also did something Sampson has wanted to do ever since we moved up here. We went to the Mallard Creek Church Barbeque and picked up barbeque for dinner.

Sampson is becoming more self-sufficient every day.

He shared with me today that he won't be able to rest until his story is published. I wondered if this was God's influence. I called Mom and asked if she would talk to a friend of hers who owns a public relations company. She had offered to help us get started and give us some advice, so I figured that would be a good place to start.

I've been reluctant about seeing the story in print because I've always felt there was more to the story than just the accident. True, it was God's grace that granted us the opportunity to share this amazing story, but there was so much more healing, learning, and leaning on God to come. Shouldn't we wait? Is this God's nudge or simply Sampson's desire to tell his story?

*****

A week later we took another trip, but this time it was a trip to the Burn Center in Augusta, GA. It was time for another checkup with Dr. Hassan.

After checking me over and asking how I was coming along, he said he was pleased with my progress and said my burns were healing just as they should be. Since he was so pleased, I decided to ask him if I could go back to work.

At first he said he wanted me to stay home for a couple more weeks. Then I explained to him that my job wasn't extremely physical and that I would be riding in my truck most of the time. He reconsidered and decided I could return to work in one week.

I was one happy man!

Before we left the Burn Center, we visited 4West for our last time. We said our hellos and hugged all the nurses who were working that day that we knew. They seemed glad to see us as always, and we were just as glad to see them. That is one special group of people. Nurses who work with burn patients are truly remarkable. What they deal with on a day-to-day basis is mind-boggling. I was so caught up in my world of building highways that I never thought much about what other people do for a living.

This accident has opened my eyes.

There are many caring people out there who get very little recognition for what they do, and since my accident I have made it a point to try and recognize the importance of everyone and the jobs they perform.

And I make sure to thank every person that helps me.

Because of my trips to 4West, I've also come to realize just how fortunate I am in another way. Sure, I was burned and now I only have one arm, but my burns aren't horribly disfiguring and it was my decision to cut off my arm. And even though I was trapped with no other way out, I made the decision to cut my arm off so I could live. And somewhere in my subconscious I knew that if I survived, life would be different.

I can't help but think about those who don't have the opportunity to make a choice. For example, an acquaintance of mine was riding his motorcycle one minute, and woke up hours later in a hospital with no arms. He had no warning. He had no choice. What he experienced was a crash, darkness, and then the reality that his arms had been amputated. Then there are those who look in the mirror every day of their lives and see a constant reminder of the agony of disfiguring flames. People forced to live their lives enduring the stares of well-meaning people.

Losing a limb is traumatic enough when you know what's coming and make the conscious decision to face life without that limb and some scars can be covered with skin grafts or clothing and never be a source of emotional pain. I can only imagine how devastating it must be for those who suffer from injuries much worse than mine where there was no choice involved.

God bless all who have come and gone from Augusta Burn Center's 4West; the wonderful staff, nurses, and doctors who truly care for their patients, and for people everywhere who are going through difficult times as they deal with injuries and health issues.

*****

I couldn't wait to get back home to call my boss, Brian Webb, to let him know my doctor had released me to return to work in one week. When I told him the news, he was shocked. But even though I had been cleared, he told me to take off until the first of the year. I reminded him that was two months from now and that I was ready to return right now. So he met me halfway and said that I could return after the week was over as long as I agreed to work half days and not jump right in and start making a lot of decisions.

I agreed.

I was so excited that I was going back to work. No more standing in front of the dining room window watching all the neighbors going to work while I stayed at home going stir crazy. And Lee Ann was excited too. She had been out of work with me the whole time so she could stay home and take care of me. What a strong, dedicated wife I have. She is my inspiration. I've always heard that behind every good man, there is a great woman, and I'm living proof. When I was stuck in that corn picker, I thought that I would never see her again, and that made me even more determined to get free no matter what it took.

That night I called my father-in-law to tell him and my mother-in-law the good news. They were both pleased for me because they knew how much I wanted to get back to work. Evidently Keith thought if I was well enough to go back to work, then I was well enough to play. He asked me if I wanted to go duck scouting with him the next day down in the Santee swamps near Sumter, South Carolina. We had hunted together for over twenty years, and I wasn't about to stop just because I was missing an arm, so I said yes.

The next day I made the ninety minute drive from our house in North Carolina to his down in South Carolina by myself. This was my first time driving by myself since the accident, so I was very careful. By the time I arrived at Keith's house he was ready to go. He had already packed the duck boat and hitched it to the truck. Helen had made us some sandwiches for the trip.

The drive to the boat landing was about an hour and I talked Keith's ear off all the way there. This was the first time I had someone other than Lee Ann to really talk to. I told him that I still couldn't believe I put my hand inside the running corn picker.

He agreed it probably wasn't the best idea I ever had.

When we arrived at the boat landing the water was lower than normal due to a drought the Carolinas had experienced for almost two years. It was so low we had to use paddles to move the boat along until we were in water deep enough to put the motor down. While he dropped the motor and locked it in place, I looked over on the bank and couldn't believe what I saw.

There were at least ten alligators sunning themselves on the bank. Keith had seen alligators down there before, but I hadn't. That was a first for me.

All around us the leaves had begun to change colors, and the water was so calm I was caught up in the beauty of everything around me. Red, brown, gold, amber, and a dozen similar fall colors were reflected in the water. Although it was a beautiful fall day, we weren't able to do any real duck scouting because the water was too low to get back into the swampy areas we really enjoyed hunting.

We stopped and ate our lunch on a river bank, then started back to the boat landing. Once again we saw more alligators lying on the river banks. We concluded that with no water in the swamp, all the alligators had come out to the river. I had hunted this area for twenty years and had never seen an alligator. I don't mind telling you I was really scared. As we idled slowly down the river in Keith's fourteen-foot aluminum Jon boat, I was thinking about all the times I had been duck hunting, standing there in my waders in water up to my chest.

I'm glad I didn't know there were alligators sharing the water with me.

I looked toward the shore and watched as an alligator longer than our boat slip into the water. I started looking around frantically, but I couldn't see where it went. When I realized I had my left hand on the side of the boat, I pulled it back inside. I only had one arm now, and all I could see was that gator sneaking up beside the boat and biting off my only other arm.

CHAPTER 9

Back to work.

My boss still wasn't sure I should be coming back to work until January, but I was bound and determined to get back and get on with building the roadway project I had started. He had originally moved another superintendent, Raymond Foster (everybody called him "Shorty"), over from one of our other projects to fill in for me while I was out. Fortunately, Shorty and I have known each other for years, so I knew the project had been in good hands.

"Sampson, my concern is not about when you come back to work," Brian had said. "I just want to make sure you're healthy and ready to come back physically, and I'm willing to wait until the first of the year to give you plenty of time to recuperate. But if you feel like you are ready to come back, I have a few temporary conditions."

Brian insisted that Shorty would make all the decisions, and I would only work half days for the first week I was back. I agreed to the conditions over the phone because I knew that was the only way I'd be going back to work this soon. I wasn't thrilled about it, but I could live with the decision. And as it turns out, it was a wise move on Brian's part.

I spent my first day back at work riding around with Shorty and sharing my story with coworkers and subcontractors. Most of them had only heard bits and pieces of the story, and they all wanted to know what really happened. Just like any other work place, there were a lot of rumors going around about what had happened or hadn't happened. How it happened. How I got out. So I told my story to anyone who wanted to hear it.

Who would have thought I could be so exhausted just from telling my story? But I was. By the time I got home, I was wiped out and I wondered if I had gone back to work too soon. I almost called Brian Webb to tell him he was right and that I needed to take some more time off before coming back. It had been two months since my accident, and I was weaker than

I realized. So when I got home I went straight to the couch and slept the rest of the day. The second day was a repeat of the first. Still, I never let on how tired I was, not even to Lee Ann. She had gone back to work too, and I know she must have been glad to get a break after two months of taking care of me.

My second week back to work was also the week of Thanksgiving, and we only worked three days. But I worked eight hours each of those days. Shorty also began to let me make some decisions. The plan was for him to go back to his project after we returned from Thanksgiving break. On Wednesday, Brian took everyone on the project out to lunch. Thirty workers joined us as he thanked Shorty for looking after the project while I recovered from my accident. He commended everybody who was involved in keeping things running smoothly and keeping the project on track while I was out. Then he announced that I would be coming back to work full-time on Monday, and I would once again be in charge.

Before we started eating Brian asked Kelly Webb, one of our foremen who was also a preacher, if he would bless the food. He prayed a moving prayer, and one of the things that really touched me was when he thanked God for answering his prayer that I would be returned to good health and be able to come back to work. I was learning that having others pray for me was a humbling experience. And a powerful one.

He was not the only one who had shared those sentiments with me that week and a half that I had been back at work. It seemed like everybody had been praying for my family and me. These were the same people who had worked with me for years, but I had no idea about their relationship with God. Once again God was showing me what I had missed by being more focused on the job and less focused on the people doing the job.

*****

Friday, October 26 … Day 46

Sampson read my journal today, and he became very emotional. Wow, I sure didn't expect that. I believe he said he had "rivers flowing from his eyes." It seems to be getting harder and harder to accomplish any major tasks these days. Our days are broken up into so many stops and starts.

Sampson's "first" for today was driving to the 601 job site in his company truck by himself. He left around 9 a.m. I washed some clothes and got the thank you notes written when Sampson Jr. came home. We talked for a while, then he showed me some information on a rifle he had been researching. After that we had lunch.

When Sampson got home, he was drained. It must have been all that talking and the emotions of being back with the guys. The 601 crew took him to lunch. He took his meds and a nap. I took this time to read and relax. When Sampson awoke he was ready to do some chores. We piddled and then decide to go out to dinner. We had dinner at a Mexican restaurant in Harrisburg, relaxed, and had a lovely evening. God continues to bless us!

*****

Saturday, October 27 … Day 47

Off to the farm for the weekend. Sampson drove the truck down to South Carolina today. He is becoming more and more comfortable being behind the wheel. Steve, Colt, and Joyce met us at the farm. The first thing on the "To Do" list was clean up the barn and the barnyard. Our friends and family had left behind a little mess when they were here a couple of weeks ago harvesting the corn, but considering what all they had done, a little mess is no big deal. We moved the corn picker wagon from under the barn to the yard. Then we raked up the shucks and cobs, picked up trash, and filled a trailer with junk and trash to take to the landfill. Steve, Colt, and Joyce were a big help, and they got to spend some quality time with Sampson.

Later, Sampson treated us all to lunch at his favorite lunch spot, Triangle Subs, in Camden. Then we made a trip to Lowe's and purchased pine needles and some boards to complete a railing for one of the deer stands. Everyone helped spread the straw, and we enjoyed the rest of the cool fall day just soaking up the sun and walking around the pond. It is wonderful to share our beautiful place with friends and family. I love watching Sampson. It is amazing how much patience he has. Everything he does he has to find a new way to do it. Not once have I heard "I can't" come out of his mouth. My heart hurts to see how hard some things are for him, but his cheerful, positive attitude shakes me right out of any kind of pity or dark thoughts I may have. Sampson is truly an *amazing person. It is also wonderful to still have my husband to share life with. God truly meant it for good, and we will come from it stronger, more faithful, and energized to do His work. Thank you, God!*

*****

Sunday, October 28 ... Day 48 through Saturday, November 3 ... Day 55

These are the last of my journal entries. Keeping a journal has served its purpose, although I will miss making my daily entries. Writing in a journal has been a tool I used to force myself to stop and take time to be with God. This is a difficult thing to do when you are caring for others. I am a very private person and when I was journaling I never dreamed these entries would be shared or published. It is my belief that journaling was my saving grace as I nursed and cared for Sampson. I felt lead by God to share these entries so that if you are dealing with a similar situation you too might try journaling. Taking the time to journal allowed me to meditate on the day, remember the precious gift God had given me (more time with Sampson), and to give God thanks.

Sunday, Sampson and I went to Liberty Hill Presbyterian Church and met with Mom and Dad's neighbor, Debbie Elliott. Debbie is an entrepreneur who has her own communications company "Talk" out of Wilmington, NC. Debbie gave us a lot of information about what we could expect to happen once our story had been introduced to the media and educated us about things we would have never considered. Telling ones story is not a simple, uncomplicated task. Out of the goodness of her heart she didn't charge us a dime for her time and the consultation. She was wonderful. Then we had lunch with my parents. It was a beautiful day.

Monday, we went to Augusta from the farm. Sampson drove. Everything checked out great, so we don't have to go back until January.

Tuesday, Sampson went to physical therapy and occupational therapy for the first time and got great news. There is no real adhesive capsulitis. That's doctor language for a frozen shoulder. It generally happens when the shoulder becomes painful and loses motion because of inflammation. Sampson has some significant stiffness, and if he does some simple stretching and rotating exercises, he'll soon get his full range of motion back.

The other good news: additional occupational therapy won't be necessary because the therapist said his hand looks great.

Wednesday, Sampson went into the swamps with my dad. It was a long day for Sampson, filled with lots of driving and being outdoors. I got a lot of paperwork and laundry done. It feels as if things are getting back to normal.

Thursday, Sampson went back to physical therapy, and then he went to Blythe's main office, and then rode around the job site. While he was gone, I went to the grocery store. When we got home, his mom and his sister Gale had arrived from Kentucky. They plan to stay until Monday.

Friday, Sampson took his mom and sister to the Billy Graham Library and I went to Montreat, North Carolina with the Rocky River Presbyterian Church group for a long-planned retreat. I spent a good part of Saturday meeting people from the church I had never met before.

The theme for the retreat was "As God Sees Us — Making Peace with Our Bodies." I needed to be reminded that I am fearfully and wonderfully made in God's image, woven in my mother's womb. It was a particularly good subject since I am struggling with a gain of 14 pounds during these eight-weeks since Sampson's accident. I know what my major weakness is, but can't seem to shake it. It's the thorn in my side, and God knows it.

It's Saturday evening and we are preparing for meditation using a Labyrinth and prayer stations. My experience can best be summed up in this way: I've walked the walk. It made me feel at peace. I felt a sense of not being alone in my needs and weaknesses as I passed shoulder-to-shoulder with others knowing that they too were crying out to God. I remembered all I was thankful for, tried to be still and receive, got to the middle of the circle and let it all go to be resolved, and walked out in peace. It was a longer journey than I thought.

CHAPTER 10

Every year at Thanksgiving, the *Chronicle-Independent* newspaper produces a special issue, and that year my story made the front page. I couldn't believe it when my mother-in-law, who works at the newspaper, brought me fifty copies. I remembered that while I was in the hospital, people kept telling me that I needed to share my story. I had promised her that I would let the newspaper she works for have the story first. They were eager to publish my story and sent Martin L. Cahn to interview me and photographer, Mark Griggs to take the pictures. I figured they would probably print a paragraph or two about the accident and that would be the end of it, so I never expected to see over two pages. When I saw that the editors had dedicated this whole issue to my story, I couldn't believe it.

Lee Ann and I wanted to buy a full-page advertisement to thank all of our friends and family by name for helping us through the previous two months. The *Chronicle-Independent* wouldn't hear of it. They did the ad for us at no charge. The picture on the front page showed Lee Ann, Sampson Jr., and me on the front porch of our cabin at the farm. With the pond in the background, it was a beautiful view. They had another picture of me standing beside Doug Spinks with a beautiful Carolina blue sky in the background. Later that year the story and the photo of Doug and me won special awards.

The next day we received many calls from TV, radio, and newspaper reporters wanting to interview me. It was a crazy time. First, WIS TV in Columbia, South Carolina wanted to do a story. So I told them that wouldn't be a problem as long as they were willing to come to the farm to shoot the interview. They sent a reporter, Dan Tordjman and his cameraman Brian, both of whom made the whole interview process enjoyable and practically stress free.

That was the first of what would become many TV interviews. In fact, I did four more interviews with Dan and Brian over the next six months, in addition to all the other TV interviews I had. At one point they even came to my house and did a story on how I was recovering, and later did a story on the rehabilitation of my shoulder and use of my prosthetic arm. The last interview we did together was one about me planting corn in the spring of 2008.

The day after the original WIS interview, Doug Spinks called and said that the people from the *Today Show* wanted to do an interview with the two of us at the farm.

The *Today Show*. I didn't see that one coming.

I asked him if he wanted to do it, and he said he did. So he called the producer back and said we would be happy to do it. Later that Saturday, they called me to confirm and told me they wanted to change the interview from Sunday to Monday morning because they would have over twenty million people watching the show on a Monday and felt this story demanded that audience.

Twenty million?

I didn't see that one coming either.

Once again, I said yes without even thinking. Lee Ann and I left the farm on Sunday morning after church and went back to our home in North Carolina to get clean clothes and call our bosses to let them know we wouldn't be at work on Monday. We had only been back to work a week and a half, and already we were asking for time off. Amazingly neither one of our bosses had a problem with our request. We drove back to the farm that evening since the interview was scheduled so early.

The film crew was scheduled to arrive at 5:30 a.m. to set everything up, and they were there right on time. I hadn't slept well the night before, so I was already up and ready well before they arrived. All I could think about was twenty million people watching me on television. That and wondering what kind of questions the *Today Show* host was going to ask me.

While they were setting up, I asked the film crew if they wanted some coffee. They all did. Two of them had driven down from Charlotte, and the producer had driven in from Virginia on Sunday and spent the night in Camden, about twelve miles from the farm. So they were ready for a cup. I left the farm and drove up to the Bojangles' in Kershaw and brought back coffee and biscuits for everybody.

By the time I returned, even though it was still dark everywhere else, it looked like it was about 10 a.m. at the farm because of all the big lights they had set up in the field while I was gone. There was a huge truck off to one side with a satellite unit on top and cables running in every direction.

Doug arrived with some of his friends from the Kershaw Fire Department where he is a firefighter. It was almost daylight. The crew started putting microphones on us and getting the IFB earpieces in place, getting us ready for the show. At one point I said, "Hey Doug, if I pass out during this interview, would you save me a second time?" At first he just laughed. Then when I told him how many people were going to be watching us, he was suddenly just as nervous as I was.

Since I leave for work early, I don't watch a lot of TV in the mornings. In fact, I couldn't remember ever having watched the *Today Show,* so I had no idea who I was going to be talking to. But I would find out soon. Twenty minutes to be exact.

The producer came over and told us we would be interviewed by Matt Lauer. A minute later she positioned us the way she wanted us, and the next thing I knew I heard people from New York talking in my ear. They were doing a sound check.

I remember thinking, "This is wild. Here I am with the man who saved my life, standing in front of the corn picker where I almost burned to death, and in a few minutes I'm going to tell my story to twenty million people all over the world." I couldn't believe God was going to use me to remind people not to do dumb things, like putting your hand in a running corn picker, and to tell people all over the world that there is a God. A loving, caring, grace-filled God who is always there for us, even in the most drastic circumstances.

God's funny like that.

The countdown began: three, two, one, and then we heard Matt talking to us. We couldn't see him though. All we could see was the camera.

It wasn't going to be as bad as I thought it would.

Matt started out asking me about the accident, and when I got to the part about blood shooting out about three feet from the stump of my arm as I ran to my truck, Matt reminded me that most of the viewers were still eating breakfast.

Oops.

Too much information.

I apologized and kept going. No one had told me what I could or could not say, so I was just telling him what happened. After a few more questions from Matt, he asked me if I wanted him and some of his buddies to come to the farm and help destroy the corn picker.

I laughed and said, "Sure, come on down."

Later I realized that he didn't get it. It wasn't the corn picker that caused me to lose my arm. It was a single, stupid, split-second decision that I made that caused me to lose my arm. I realized that, from then on, I had to make that point clear.

After that interview, things were wild for the next two weeks. Every day I was doing radio interviews with stations all over the country. I did live TV interviews with CNN and FOX, and I also did a live interview on a morning talk show called *Sunrise Australia* in Sidney, Australia. We did that one by using a live hookup in a production studio in Charlotte. I never saw the person I was talking to, but they sure did speak differently.

Newspapers and radio stations from all over the country wanted interviews. My favorite radio interview was a station out of Buffalo, New York. They were holding a contest called "Balls of Steel."

I won.

I was getting better at interviews, and in every interview I made it clear that were it not for the grace of God, I wouldn't be talking to them. Some of the interviewers would cut the interview short as soon as I brought God into the story, so I made sure after learning the hard way that the most crucial element of the story would not be left out again.

Part of that learning the hard way included a documentary for the TV series, *I Survived*. That one took eight hours to film, and they filmed it at the farm. When I received the copy of the story, they had cut out everything I said about God. I understand that programs like that have to be edited, but the fact that they edited out everything I said about God's part in my story made me mad. They excluded the most important part.

Without God's grace, sure, it's still a good story. But it's not the *whole* story, and the whole story needed to be told.

CHAPTER 11

It had been over three months since the accident, and while I wasn't feeling 100 percent, I was getting stronger. The time had finally come to start looking for a company that made prosthetic devices.

On the surface it sounds like a pretty simple thing, but little did we know, we were in for a real education.

*****

No one prepared us for what we were about to encounter. In fact, we were given very little direction on how to go about getting a prosthetic device. We were told we needed to see an arm specialist, so we received a referral from our family physician and made an appointment with an orthopedic doctor. We assumed the doctor would talk to us about what was available, what he would recommend for Sampson's needs, and then get started on the process of getting him a prosthesis. When the doctor came into the room, he gave Sampson a funny look. With what we learned later, he must have been thinking "And what am I supposed to do for this guy? He has already had his surgery." As it turns out, we didn't even need to see him. I was so disappointed. Talk about a letdown.

*****

After the orthopedic doctor looked at my arm, he said the surgery they had performed looked good and my arm had healed well. According to him, there seemed to be plenty of natural padding at the end of the bone, so I should be able to wear a prosthetic device without any problem. So we asked him, since I had been given the okay to get a prosthetic arm, how we would go about choosing a prosthetic company. He was able to recommend one near the hospital. So Lee Ann and I left his office and went straight there. We had come to get the ball rolling, and that's what we intended to do.

We walked in, and there was only one person working there. So I gave him the prescription for a prosthetic arm and said, "Hey, I need a new arm."

He didn't get the joke. In fact, he seemed to be lost and in shock. He told us that to his knowledge they had only created one arm because they mostly provide prosthetic legs. He told us that Charlotte is in the center of the "diabetic beltway," and most of their customers were older people who had lost their feet or legs due to complications from diabetes. Then he told us that most people who lose arms do so around more central states like Iowa, Indiana, and other farming states.

Well, it was educational, but I was disappointed.

I looked at Lee Ann and told her I didn't want someone making an arm for me if they didn't know what they were doing. So we left and went home.

I don't know what I was thinking. How hard did it have to be? I figured you would just go to some place like Arm-mart, look around, and pick out an arm. And nobody told us any different. In fact, nobody told us anything at all. So how were we supposed to know what to do? How is anybody in that situation supposed to know what to do?

The first thing we did when we got home was to get on the internet and look for prosthetic companies in our area. Then we made calls and set up appointments.

Later that day Alice Williams came to visit us again. She had heard that I was not working my fingers, and that they were becoming drawn up and stiff. As an occupational therapist at a local rehabilitation center, she knew how important it was to get the flexibility back in my hand as soon as possible. She had come specifically to talk to me and show me several ways I could begin my own physical therapy. She gave my hand a deep tissue massage as she provided information about what was happening with my hand. I told her about our frustrating day trying to track down a prosthetic arm, as she continued to work her magic as she stretched my fingers and massaged my hand.

Afterwards she told us about a neighbor of hers who owns a prosthetic business that deals in arms and legs. They had been in business for over 50 years, and she highly recommended them. After she left we got back online and found their web site. Their company was exactly what we were looking for.

Once again my spirits had been lifted by the possibility of getting a prosthetic arm. The next day we called Faith Prosthetic and Orthotic Services, Inc., and they told us to come right then. We met with a prosthetist named Steve Overcash, who went into great detail about what was available and how the process begins. We also discovered that the $10,000 annual maximum coverage our insurance provided would cover only the very basic manual-type arm. I was curious and asked if he had an arm I could see and maybe try on. I am sure he was laughing to himself as he told me no and further explained that each device was individually fitted. Arms were not Steve's specialty, but Sam Brouillette, one of the members of his group, was known around Charlotte for the work he had done with arms.

Now we were getting somewhere. The next day we went straight to Sam's office.

After telling Sam my story, we got down to business. He started measuring my arm and then told me, although the surgeon did a great job at providing plenty of cushion at the end of my nub, my arm was too long for ideal use of a prosthetic. Then he mentioned the possibility of an additional surgery to shorten the arm.

I couldn't believe what I was hearing. And I let him know in no uncertain terms that surgery was not an option.

"More surgery? No. I've had more than enough surgery already. I've had all the surgery I can stand, and I am not about to have any more on that arm. So you're just going to have to work with what you've got."

Now I understood why the doctors at the Burn Center worked so hard to save my elbow. If they could have saved it, all I would need is a forearm and hand, but since the amputation was above the elbow the prosthetic arm would need an elbow and a piece that goes all the way up to the shoulder. Sam's concern was that the humerus bone of my arm may have been left a little too long to fit comfortably into the sleeve and that it may make the prosthetic arm noticeably longer than my other arm. He was telling me that I may need to have the humerus shortened for a better fit and symmetry. No, I'd already performed one surgery on it, and then the doctors performed a few more surgeries on it. As far as I was concerned, that was plenty.

Sam could tell he had upset me, and he quickly started taking more measurements. After a few calculations, he looked up and said the words I wanted to hear.

"Mr. Parker, I can make it work."

After we finished the rest of the preliminaries, he took us on a tour of the lab where they mold, paint, sand, and create the outer shell for the prosthetic arms and legs. There were arms, legs, feet, and hands hanging everywhere. It was hard to believe that there were that many people in the area who wore prosthetic limbs.

It was fascinating, but it also gave Lee Ann an uneasy feeling. She told me after we left that she felt like she was seeing parts of people. And not that she was squeamish. That wasn't it. She said it was more of a personal thing because she knew deep inside that each limb represented someone who had a story to share.

We had enough for one day and were glad it was time to go. With my next appointment made for fitting, we were out of there.

CHAPTER 12

Back at Faith Prosthetics, Sam started the process with a bucket of plaster and several packages of bandages. He began by wrapping what was left of my right arm. He wrapped from just under my armpit to the end of my right arm, which ends just above the elbow. I call it my nub. Then they soaked the bandages in plaster and created a mold.

After the mold was made we sat down to look at all the different options for my arm and calculate what my insurance would pay for, and what we could afford to pay. While we were running the figures, I asked him how long this would take to make my arm. He said four to six weeks.

Man, here we go again. I thought I would have an arm in a couple of days. In fact, I thought I would have an arm before I went back to work. But it took longer than I had planned on.

After weeks of going back and forth for fittings, Sam was finally satisfied with the results, but he was still waiting for the parts to come in that would allow him to make the arm useable. By this time I had become accustomed to having the use of only one arm. I was beginning to think I didn't even need a prosthetic arm and that getting one was a lot of trouble and money. I was getting by with one arm just fine.

Two months later the arm was finally ready. I could not wait to try it out. I put the arm on, and my first thought was that this thing is heavy and bulky. After a few adjustments we got it to work properly, and by the end of the day I was using the arm. It was nothing like I thought it would to be. I told Lee Ann that I had gone without an arm for months and that I really didn't need a prosthetic arm. She was not happy with that at all. So, I told her I would wear it and make every attempt to get used to it.

For several weeks I carried my arm around with me in my truck and only put it on if I needed to do something that took the use of a helper hand. I didn't wear it to physical therapy while they were working on my frozen shoulder. One day I needed to get some work done to the arm, and

I carried the arm instead of wearing it to the prosthetic office.

Just like Lee Ann, they were not happy that I was not wearing my arm.

At that point Sam knew I needed to get motivated and serious about using my prosthetic arm. He made an appointment for me with Dr. Sharon K. Kanelos, a physiatrist in Charlotte who was board certified in Physical Medicine and Rehabilitation. He explained to me that, as a physiatrist, she works to treat the whole person, not just the problem area. Because of that he thought she would be able to help me with this major change in my life. I can be hard-headed at times, but was willing to see what Dr. Kanelos had to say.

I went to Dr. Kanelos's office the next day, and she already knew a lot about me. I sat in her office for an hour and a half while she drilled into me that I needed to start wearing my prosthetic arm. She said if I didn't wear the arm and use it that my left arm would be worn out in less than ten years.

"Why aren't you using it?" she asked.

"I just don't want to put it on."

"Sampson, that's not a reason. That's an excuse. The thing is, with lower prosthetics, people use them primarily to walk. But an upper body prosthetic plays a different part.

"It doesn't really mimic hand function because those movements are so intricate. What you have acts more as an aid than a substitute. And when you wear the prosthetic, not only are you more balanced, but it also relieves some of the pressure on your other shoulder. That's why if you don't start wearing it, you will wear out that shoulder in the next ten years."

She was right. Everything I was doing, I did using my left arm.

"Tell me," she said, "what do you do when you get up in the morning?"

"I put my pants on and then my shirt and socks and shoes and cap, and then I go to work."

"That's fine," she said. "Now I want you to add one more step. I want it to become part of your daily routine. Put on your pants, put on your arm, put on your shirt, put on your socks and shoes, then put your hat on and go to work."

I started to protest again, but she stopped me.

"Just put your arm on. It's a process. And after a few weeks, it will be a habit. Make it an integrated part of the day … part of a routine. You need to give it a fair trial."

She must have said that last part a dozen times. And like I've said before, I am a little hard-headed. But I finally got the message.

The fact is, I needed to hear what she told me, and thanks to her persistence, I finally got the message loud and clear. I am so thankful that she took the time with me and made me realize how important it was that I start using the prosthetic arm. She played a major part in my road to recovery. A much more important part than I originally thought s he could.

*****

After a lot of practice, I began to get the hang of my new arm. The ultimate challenge was to see if I could operate equipment. So since my attitude is usually "full steam ahead," one day I jumped up on a small dozer at work and started pushing dirt. It was difficult at first because I had to operate the blade lever with my prosthetic arm. The problem was that the hook, which takes the place of my right hand, kept slipping off the handle. I couldn't grip the handle like I was used to. But I was determined to find a way around the problem because I was determined to operate this machine.

As I worked on acquiring the new skills it would take for me to get back in the saddle, so to speak, I thought, "Here I am in the middle of Interstate 85, running a John Deere 550 bulldozer with all these people going by me, and the only thing between me and them is a concrete barrier wall." But I was having a ball.

When the dozer operator returned from lunch he couldn't believe that I was running his machine. He gave me a thumbs up and told me I did a great job. I felt so good after that, I was determined to try my favorite piece of equipment: a track excavator. But where the bulldozer had been a challenge, this could be even worse because it is more difficult to operate.

But I got on the machine and started working everything out. The

135

problem this time was that the forearm of the prosthetic arm kept slipping out of the position it needed to be in for me to dump a bucket of dirt.

As I thought about the problem, I remembered there was a screw on the elbow that would tighten the forearm. Once I tightened that, the forearm stayed in place, and I was able to operate the excavator. Granted, I wasn't operating it the way I once had, but I was still operating it, and doing a pretty decent job.

I was actually getting back to doing the things I enjoyed.

And without the help of the prosthetic arm, I would never have been able to do it.

As the weeks and months went by I continued to grow stronger and continued to adapt to my new arm by finding different ways to do the things I have always done.

*****

In the spring of 2008 it was time to plant corn, and I was back on my tractor plowing the fields. I bought a used tractor so Sampson Jr. could have one of his own to plow with, and that made it even more fun. Whenever we would pass each other on the tractors, we would give each other a thumbs up. With two tractors and two operators, it didn't take us long as it had in the past to plow our fields in preparation for planting corn. Once we had the fields plowed Sampson Jr. dragged the ground smooth, while I came along right behind him and planted corn.

I couldn't believe it. I was farming again.

The rhythm of life was getting back to normal.

*****

Next came fishing season. I thought operating a rod and reel would be tough, and it was at first. But because the staff at Faith Prosthetics knew how much I loved to fish, they had given me a special adaptor that was interchangeable with my hook. They also gave me a special fishing rod that connects to the adaptor. And while it was a kind gesture, it was a little too cumbersome and difficult to use. As much as I appreciated Faith's generosity, I eventually took it off and just used my claw. I was able to hold the rod fine. The only difference was that reeling in the line wasn't quite as smooth as it had once been, but that wasn't a big deal.

The first fish I caught using my prosthetic arm was a three pound bass I pulled out of the pond on the farm. I also realized that using a prosthetic arm had its advantages. One good thing about having a claw for a hand is that you can reach into the mouth of a bass to get your hook out without getting your fingers all nasty.

As I adjusted to this new tool, I realized just how awesome it was to be able to do all the things I loved. Just another thing I thank God for every day.

*****

Many months later, after the Rowan County I85 project was completed and I was assigned permanently to the Union County 601 project, Sampson Jr. worked on the job with me during his summer college break. He learned to operate dozers, rollers, and pans, and also had the opportunity to work with the field engineers in the site office. He hated being inside, but I wanted him to experience both aspects of building a highway.

At lunch time we would sometimes leave the job site and drive around the area and look at all the farm land. We scouted areas for deer and ducks and would watch the farmers as they harvested their wheat on big John Deere combines. And we both wanted to operate one.

While on the 601 project I was introduced to one of the largest farm owners in the state of North Carolina, Marion Cox, owner of Cox Brothers Farms. Marion and his lovely wife, Delano, along with Marion's brother Bobby and their children and grandchildren operate and farm about 12 thousand acres of corn, soybeans and wheat. In addition, they also raise hogs and turkeys. I truly admire and respect Marion and I am honored to call him my friend. In fact, I hold the entire Cox family in high regard and I am so thankful to have met them all.

I had ridden with Marion and Bobby on their big John Deere combine, and I wanted Sampson Jr. to have the opportunity to ride on one. So Marion told me to bring him over during our lunch break one day and he would be glad to take Sampson Jr. for a ride.

Sampson Jr. couldn't believe it when we pulled up to the combine and I told him Marion was going to give him ride. He was like a kid in a candy store. He got to ride for an hour. Then I had to get him back to the job. On the way back, we talked about how awesome the combine was, and we both agreed we were going to buy a John Deere combine one day to pick corn on our farm.

Times like that with my son are priceless, and I thank God for them every day. How blessed I am to get a second chance.

CHAPTER 13

Around Christmas of 2007, the *Today Show* director called to tell me that my story was one of their top ten stories of the year. I was shocked. They wanted me to come to New York to do a live interview with Matt Lauer, but this time I didn't say yes right away. I thought and prayed about it for several days. I talked it over with Lee Ann and Sampson Jr., then called the director back and said I would do the interview and asked them if they would also include accommodations for my wife, son, and his girlfriend at the time, Heather.

They had no problem with my request, and they took care of everything. We flew out of Charlotte on a Thursday morning, and by that afternoon, we were sitting in our rooms looking over Times Square during one of the most beautiful times of the year: Christmas. The huge tree in Times Square was even more fascinating than on TV. I couldn't believe this was happening to me.

After a restless night, I asked God to help me through this interview. I was so nervous that I was shaking, and we hadn't even left our hotel room. Sampson Jr. and I shared one room, while Lee Ann and Heather shared the other. Because Lee Ann and I weren't in the same room I wasn't able to share how I was feeling with her. And there was no way I was going to tell Sampson Jr. Then again, I knew what he would have told me. He would have told me to "get tough."

When the time came, we all walked over to the Rockefeller Center on our own. No one told us that they would be picking us up. I am glad we walked because we were able to go around the crowd that had already gathered to watch the show from the street.

We came to the fence that was used to keep people away from the building and allowed the *Today Show* crew to come into the street where they do the outside live slot. From there, we made it to the front door. The guard told us we couldn't enter the building. I told him who I was, and that

I was supposed to be on the show that morning. He made a quick call, and less than a minute later, a lady came out and took us right in and up to the holding area where they prep guests.

What a building. This had to be the nicest building I had ever been in. I thought I had been nervous back at the hotel, but that was *nothing* compared to what I felt at this point. Now my legs were shaking and my voice was starting to crack just talking to Lee Ann, Sampson Jr., and Heather. They all tried to keep me distracted by talking about anything and everything except the upcoming interview.

This wasn't like the first interview where I was in my own territory. Just me, a camera and a few people. I was way out of my league.

They introduced me to one of their makeup artists, and told me she would touch me up. I laughed and told them I was fine. I had shaved and washed my hair that morning, and I thought I looked presentable. She convinced me, however, that she could touch up the shiny spots and adjust my hair just a bit in order for me to look my best.

How could I resist?

While she was putting makeup on me, the makeup person at the chair beside me was putting makeup on Bryant Gumbel. He never looked in my direction, so I didn't even know who he was until I asked the lady working on me.

Once the makeup artist finished, we continued to wait in the holding room where they provided coffee, juice, doughnuts, and all sorts of other morning foods. Lee Ann, Sampson Jr., and Heather enjoyed the spread, but I was too nervous to even think about eating. There was a large, flat screen TV in the room with the *Today Show* playing. Bryant Gumbel was already on the air.

While we watched the show, the former Miss Kentucky, Tara Conner, walked in and sat down next to me. I couldn't believe I was in the same room as her. Because of her struggles with drugs and alcohol, and the fact that she had turned her life around, her story had made headlines. Since I am from Kentucky, and knowing she was from there too, we immediately hit it off. We talked about the areas we grew up in and how beautiful it is there. She asked me why I was on the show, and I told her what I had begun calling "The Short Version" of my story.

She was close to tears, and she had not even heard the meat of the story. I told her how nervous I was to be on live TV with Matt. Then she started telling me how it works and said to just look at Matt and not to think of anything else. She also advised me to only answer the questions he asked and to not get carried away with too many details. I thought to myself, "That is just what Lee Ann has been telling me for days". Tara didn't seem a bit nervous. She was next to be interviewed by Matt. I wished her good luck, and she was gone.

Then, it was my turn.

They took me into a big room with all of the *Today Show* crew. I walked in during a commercial while everyone was getting into their positions. I sat down and looked out through the window at the people in Times Square. Matt came over to me and shook my hand and told me he was glad to meet me, while someone put a microphone on my shirt and an earpiece in my ear. We didn't have much time to talk before the director started the countdown. At that point I didn't have time to get nervous with so many things going on all at once.

Next, I heard that familiar "Three … two … one." in my ear, and then Matt was talking to me. Oddly enough, I never once thought about those twenty million people out there watching. I just answered his questions. I didn't get a chance to thank everyone for all the prayers and support, but I did give thanks to God on national TV. To this day people still thank me for publically giving God the credit.

Matt asked me about the prosthetic arm and how it was coming along. The producer really wanted me to be wearing it, but this all happened prior to the arm being completed, so I didn't have one yet. I put a lot of pressure on Faith Prosthetics to get the arm finished before the trip to New York, but it didn't happen in time.

I explained to Matt that certain parts were on backorder, and he commented that it sounded like a person waiting on parts for a car repair.

After the interview, Matt thanked me for coming and said if he could help me out in any way to just to give him a call. He seemed very sincere. We shook hands, and I was escorted back to the waiting room. Lee Ann,

Sampson Jr., and Heather were all sitting there and had been watching me on the TV. We all sat there talking about how I did. I was glad it was over, but I wished I had more time to tell the whole story. I mostly wished I could have talked about all the people that had helped me for the last three months. Lee Ann said that that would have taken all day, and that there would soon be a time where I could do just that. Now that the interview was over, I was ready to have some fun and see the sights of New York City.

We left New York the next day (New Year's Eve), and before long we were back in our regular routine. That Sunday our preacher at Rocky River Presbyterian Church, Kyle Hite, mentioned that he had seen me on the *Today Show*. During his sermon, he thanked me for giving God the glory on national TV. Later he asked me to tell my story during church one day in the near future. I told him I would be glad to. In fact, I was looking forward to any opportunity to share the story of my firsthand experience of God's grace.

CHAPTER 14

It had been three months since my talk with Dr. Rollins, and the big day had finally arrived. In our little church in Liberty Hill, South Carolina, I was baptized. I was finally able to get off the pew and make that walk down the aisle. It was comforting to realize that I was surrounded by so many people who had been thinking about me and praying for me. I looked out over the congregation and saw the entire church, our families, and our friends. Even Doug Spinks and Karen Baker had come for the big event.

To my surprise, Lee Ann had asked to be the Lay Leader for the service. Her inspirational message and prayer brought tears to my eyes, as it did for many of the other people there that morning.

*****

I was baptized in this church on June 11, 1972. I was sixteen years old and when I accepted Jesus Christ as my personal savior He forever changed my life. Thirty-six years later, I stand here before God, with my brothers and sisters in Christ, to witness the baptism of the most beloved person in my life.

My husband.

Although his character mirrored a Christ-like person and he had professed his belief in God and Jesus, he only attended church with me on special occasions. For the sixteen years our family resided in South Carolina, Sampson insisted I church our son. So Sampson Jr. and I attended Liberty Hill Presbyterian Church. During most of our 20 years of marriage, I have sat in church pews with no husband by my side. Rarely did I harp on him to attend church, but more often I extended invitations for him to join Sampson Jr. and me. Prayer after prayer I prayed that one day he too would desire to worship alongside of us. And the day has finally arrived. Thanks be to God! Can I have an "Amen"?

Shortly after we returned home from the Burn Center in Augusta, Sampson shared with me that he wanted to be baptized and wanted to start attending church. At first I was filled with joy and excitement; my prayers had been answered.

Then for some reason I felt down and sad. Being one who truly believes in the power of prayer, I thought, "Has Sampson's horrific ordeal been the answer to my prayers?" I immediately said to myself, "You can think this and feel guilty the rest of your life … or you can just be thankful." So I decided to just be thankful, and I have given God the glory for every moment we spend together talking about God's grace, praying, and just loving life.

"From the fullness of His grace, we have all received one blessing after another." John 1:16

As I reminisced about those in our congregation, friends, and family who have suffered sickness, loss, and tragedy I remember thinking during those times, "How in the world do they manage to go on with life"

Now I know.

It is our faith in Jesus Christ that brings us through circumstances that we often deny and pray we will never experience. It is simply our belief in the Father, the Son, and the Holy Spirit that brings us the grace of God. During life's most difficult times, you may not recognize His grace; other times it will stare you right in the face. Look for it. You may be blinded by circumstance, yet His grace will surround you. Look for it, be thoughtful of it, and be thankful for it.

Sampson, here before God, our family, and our friends, I welcome you to a new life in Christ. I love you.

After a great sermon from Dr. Rollins, we all went to the farm and had lunch. While we were there I got to meet two of Doug Spinks children, and I made sure I told them what an awesome dad they had.

They both agreed.

CHAPTER 15

With a very mild winter and a warm spring, we were able to get the I-85 project finished on time. I was so proud of everyone who worked on the project with me. After three years of working together it was time for us to go our separate way and move on to the next jobs. Because of what had happened to me while on this job, there was a bond between us that would never be forgotten.

It was time to fully dedicate my time to another project that dovetailed the Rowan County I-85 job: the Union County 601 project. I had not been back to work on this project since the morning of my accident. My boss, Brian Webb, had told me to only look after the I-85 project and get it finished before returning to 601. Before the accident, I was going back and forth to both jobs. By the time I returned, they had moved some of the crews that had worked with me for years from I-85 to the 601 project. This is not the norm for the highway construction industry. There is a lot of turnover; people come and go with the start and finishing of jobs.

One of the people they moved was Terry Hensley. Terry and I go back a long ways. We've worked together for more than ten years. And since Terry is from Kentucky too, we had a unique bond. Throughout the years we did our share of fussing and feuding, but respected each other tremendously.

And now, Terry was running the 601 project in my absence.

Since the accident, I had only driven through the project on my way to the farm, so I had been a "windshield superintendent" during the last three months while finishing I-85. But on the job, I kept my thoughts to myself. But, I told Lee Ann some of what I was seeing and shared what I would be doing if I was on the job. She reminded me that everyone does things just a little differently, and the end result would still be the same. Even so, it was difficult for me to watch someone else working on my project. Even someone I liked.

The first few weeks back on the 601 project were emotional for me. I was still very weak and not 100 percent. It had only been six months since my accident, and I was going to rehabilitation twice a week. I was still unable to fully rotate my right shoulder. I had babied it for so long, afraid to move the arm that had lost its better half to that corn picker. Because of this it had become sort of stuck from not being used. I couldn't raise what was left of my right arm above my head.

After months of rehabilitation, my physical therapist finally put me on a table and physically pulled my arm back until it popped into place. First I felt it, and then we actually heard it break free. After that I was able to put my right arm all the way up and back behind my head like I could do with my left arm.

Freedom of movement at last.

It felt so good to be able to stretch my right arm, and now I could start working on how to use my prosthetic arm.

During the next three visits I worked on learning how to pick things up and put them down using the prosthetic arm's claw. The physical therapists said they were impressed with how easy it was for me to do the tasks they gave me. At one point they gave me a board with nuts and bolts, which I would have to take off and put back together. I would use my claw like a wrench and hold the nut while I turned the bolt with my left hand.

They would also have me carry things like books and plates from one place to another. I even had to put forks and knives at a table and learn to eat with my right claw. It took a lot of practice and patience to do anything with the prosthetic arm. But it has been well worth it.

Each day I am faced with simple everyday tasks and difficult new challenges that can be frustrating for people who have lost limbs. But I also begin each day with a prayer of thanks to God for giving me another chance at life. Then I use four God-given tools: attitude, patience, determination, and practice. With God's grace and these four tools, I am able to stay focused and continue to make progress toward a life of independence and normalcy.

CHAPTER 16

The fall of 2008 arrived, and once again it was time to pick corn and get ready for deer season. And in order to do that, I knew I had to buy a new corn picker because it would cost too much to repair the old one. After a little searching, I found a corn picker just like the one that had burned at the farm. Early one morning Lee Ann and I drove out to take a look at it and make sure it was in good condition.

At first, everything was fine. We checked the machine over, and I looked to make sure the various mechanisms were in good working order. On the outside it seemed fine. Now all I had to do was get the farmer who owned it to crank it up so I could make sure it was mechanically sound. I asked him if he would crank it up, and he said of course.

The machine roared to life and I just froze. That was the first time I had heard that sound since the accident. My stomach lurched, and I went cold inside. That sound, once so comforting and natural, sounded like the voice of death. In the space of a few seconds, the events of September 11 rushed back with a force I couldn't have imagined possible. Lee Ann held my hand tight, but I could barely feel it. As the machine idled, the terror was starting to build.

"Please, turn it off," I said. I had tears in my eyes, and if he had let that picker run another thirty seconds, I would probably have started sobbing and wouldn't have been able to stop. I couldn't stand it because it reminded me of the noise the rollers made as they ripped into my hand.

The sick feeling in the pit of my stomach got worse because, for one horrible moment, it was like being stuck in that machine all over again. When I regained control of myself, I told the farmer what had happened to me. He was very kind and wanted to know if there was anything at all he could do for me.

"No, I'll be fine," I said. "I just didn't expect it to affect me like that." I looked at the machine for a few seconds and then pulled myself together.

The farmer went on to tell us that at the same time as my accident, a man who farmed just across the swamp had been in the same predicament. He hadn't been so fortunate. He was discovered dead in his picker, one hand stuck in the bottom and the other hand stuck in the top side.

I felt a lump growing in my throat as I wondered, "Why me, God? Why not him? Why am I the one who lived? What is your plan for me, God?"

I didn't buy that particular corn picker, but I felt God must have sent me there for a reason. As I thought about it, I realized the lesson for me was to be aware every day of how lucky I am to have been graced with a second chance.

Not long after that experience, I found a corn picker identical to the one I had before, except it was in better condition. All the parts on this one worked. The next time I heard the sound of the corn picker, Sampson Jr. was with me. And once again the sound brought back all the memories of that September day.

Every time I picked over the spot where I lost my arm, I would get cold chills and the nerves in my right arm would act up. It felt as if fire was shooting out of what was left of my arm, and my phantom fingers were on fire. It was then that I realized that it was time to deal with it once and for all. Frustrated and yet thankful to be alive, I looked up to the sky and thanked God that I was still here doing what I love to do. To this day every time I go over that spot, I get cold chills remembering what happened. But I have made peace with the memories.

As I said earlier, corn picking season is also deer season, and I couldn't wait to get in the deer stand. It had been over two years since I had been deer hunting, and I was ready. But there was a small hitch. I had shot a few doves earlier on the opening day of dove season, but after shooting right-handed for forty-five years, I found that it was hard to keep my right eye closed. Shooting left-handed was turning out to be a big adjustment. I figured I was going to need some extra practice before I went after a buck.

The weekend before deer season opened, Sampson Jr. and I went down to the farm to sight in our rifles. After shooting a box of shells, I finally started hitting the target. And after a little more practice, I started shooting as well as Sampson Jr.

Now it was time to see if I could get a deer. Because of the accident, I had missed out on the previous deer season, so I was determined to get one this year. The next weekend I went back out to the farm to hunt. Sampson Jr. was hunting in North Carolina, so I was there by myself. As I headed up into the deer stand, I almost fell. "Oh great," I thought. "Here I am at the farm by myself again, and the last thing I need to do is get hurt." The problem was that the steps going up to the deer stand should have been replaced years ago, but I never thought about them before because I could go up with no trouble. But I was now a one-armed deer hunter who carried a gun with a helper arm.

And nothing about that scenario was safe. I needed to replace the steps and add side rails for better balance.

After that trip Sampson Jr. and I built new steps. We cut out the steps, put four posts in the ground, and anchored them with concrete. The next day, all by myself, I finished the steps leading up to the deer stand. I was elated. I was also wiped out, to say the least, but I was also proud of what we had built. Once the steps were secured, I sat down on them and cried tears of joy, because I had been thinking for a long time that I would never be able to build anything with one arm.

By that point I was covered with sweat and a little blood from a cut, but I cried out to God and thanked him for allowing me this second chance in life and for giving me the strength to build these steps on my deer stand.

While I was thanking God, I realized something. The nail gun I had used to build the steps, a gift from my in-laws for my birthday back in February, was the key. That simple piece of equipment was a great reminder for me that nothing is impossible. In that moment, I realized that almost anything is *possible*. I just had to come up with new and different ways of doing things.

Later that day Lee Ann came down to the farm, and I couldn't wait to show her the new steps. She couldn't believe that I had finished them on my own. She was so proud of me and I just embraced the moment.

With a new set of sturdy steps, I was ready. And during the next hunt, I did what all deer hunters do. I climbed into my favorite deer stand and waited. Waiting is a big part of deer hunting, and this trip was no exception.

I sat there a long time until I had finally had enough. I figured I'd move to another position. As I was getting up to climb down the steps, I looked to my left and saw a big doe standing there eating corn. I waited a few minutes, hoping to see a buck come out looking for her, but no such luck. Since it was a doe day (one of the few times it is legal to shoot a female deer), I decided to take the shot. I eased over to the door, placed my gun out of the opening, and got her in my sights.

It was about a 100-yard shot. I took a breath, released it slowly, pulled the trigger, and she dropped to the ground. I don't mind telling you, I was shaking. I waited about ten minutes before I came down out of the stand. I walked over to the deer and saw just how big she was. I was excited until I remembered one vital piece of information: I was going to have to load her into my truck.

Being a one-armed hunter had officially become a real pain.

I looked at the deer, looked toward the barn, then back at the deer. My best bet was going to be walking back to the barn to get my truck. When I got back with the truck, I put the tailgate down and tried picking up the deer. I almost had her up when I slipped and fell.

And broke the forearm on my prosthetic arm.

The arm is simply made of hard plastic, so I wasn't surprised that it broke. But that still left me with the problem of what to do. There was no way I could load the deer with one arm. And the claw normally attached to the prosthetic arm was hanging by the cable.

I drove back to the barn to see if there was anything I could use to repair the arm, and fortunately I had the all-purpose tool: duct tape.

I took the duct tape and wrapped it around the broken part of my arm. It held the arm together, but I knew I wouldn't be able to depend on the helper arm for anything strenuous. So I hooked the hay fork up to the tractor, placed a piece of plywood on the forks, and used the tractor to pick up the deer and load it into my truck.

On the way to the skin shop to get the deer processed, I was the happiest man on earth. I had just completed a successful hunt (the first in two years), and I had done it with one arm.

And a roll of duct tape.

CHAPTER 17

While I am always willing to tell my story if someone asks, there is a big difference between telling a few people in a casual setting how God saved my life and being the center of attention in a crowd of people. And while I am willing to go wherever God sends me and speak to whomever He wants me to, this was a part of God's plan that I hadn't anticipated.

*****

Sheriff Steve McCaskill (December, 2007)

I accepted my first speaking engagement from Steve McCaskill, Sheriff of Kershaw County (at the time). Steve asked me to speak at a dinner meeting he was hosting for a group of law enforcement officers. They were fifty elite officers from all over South Carolina who had gone through a rigged training course together. As part of their continued bond, each of them took turns hosting a meeting in their home towns on a quarterly basis.

I had never been in a place with so many police officers before. I was one of the few civilians present. After dinner Steve introduced me to the group, and I started telling my story. I was nervous. Other than being on stage with Doug a few times, I had never spoken in front of a group of people before … not even when I was in school. All my life I had managed to avoid any kind of public speaking.

What was I thinking?

After I told my story, the officers asked a lot of questions. At one point one of the officers asked if I would do a video to show the new recruits the importance of never giving up, no matter what type of dangerous situation they may be in. I told him I would be glad to.

Later that year they sent a full film crew to the 601 project to do the video.

*****

A&E Biography (December, 2007)

I was surprised when the producers of the A&E Biography show, *I Survived,* called and asked me about doing a segment. Yet as I thought about it, that was actually the perfect kind of show for my situation because it shows how people survived traumatic events in their lives. To this day this segment continues to run, and I have more people recognize me from this show than any other of which I have been a part.

The crew of three arrived right on time to do the shoot at our cabin on the farm. They wanted me to fly to St. Louis, Missouri to do the show, but I had only been back at work for about a month and felt I shouldn't take any more time off, so they agreed to film everything at the farm.

We talked for a while about how they wanted to set up the background, and they finally decided to shoot it from inside the cabin. Earlier in the week the producer had called to ask if I would purchase some black plastic. I thought this was strange, but didn't question her. Once they arrived, I found out that they didn't want to bring a roll of black plastic on the plane; plus, they didn't know how big my cabin was. They used the black plastic as a backdrop. Now it all made sense.

When they started setting up, I think they were surprised when they saw how small the cabin was. They even wondered out loud how they were going to shoot the film.

The producer was from California, the audio guy was from Missouri, and the cameraman was from Australia. What a diverse group of people. I asked them if they wanted to take a ride around the farm before we got started, and they all said yes. So we all got into my pickup, and I drove them around the five-acre pond, then down to my deer hunting areas and through the harvested corn field to where the burnt corn picker still sat. From there I showed them how the accident happened. When I finished, they stood there looking stunned. Next, I showed them the blood that was still on the back of the picker. They took a picture of that along with a burnt ear of corn that still lay beside my picker. Then we went back to the cabin.

They started moving everything out of the cabin onto the porch because they needed the room for their equipment. Then they draped the black plastic over all the walls and windows to make a black background, set up two big cameras in the small hallway, and put me on a stool in the middle of the room. After a couple practices and a few takes to get everything just right, the producer started asking me a lot of questions, some of which brought back some deep emotions. The interview alone lasted at least six hours.

Every time the producer asked me a question about Lee Ann, I would start to answer and felt a lump in my throat and tears running down my face. Lee Ann couldn't be with me that day because she had to work. She had missed a lot of work because of the accident — at least three months. At this point I was still weak and emotionally vulnerable. It had only been three months since my accident. However, the crew was very professional, and they always allowed me to compose myself before we moved on.

The one thing I didn't like when I received a copy of the final version that would air on TV was the fact that every word I said about God had been edited out. This was a learning experience for me, and now I make certain before I agree to do any films or interviews that God doesn't get cut out. He was the one who gave me the strength to free myself from the picker and then put the right people in place at the right time to save my life, and He will never be overlooked again if I can help it.

*****

South Carolina Farm Bureau Young Farmers and Ranchers Conference (March, 2008)

There was something special about the time I spent at the South Carolina Farm Bureau Young Farmers and Ranchers conference. They held the event at the Hyatt Regency in Greenville, South Carolina. Lee Ann and I drove down from our home in Harrisburg to enjoy the evening program and spend the night. We met a lot of the farmers and their wives during dinner, and I couldn't help but think, "This is my kind of crowd."

The next morning we were up early because I was slated to tell my story at 8 a.m. When the time came, the conference leader introduced me and I went up on stage. As I looked around at all those young faces, I thought to myself, "These guys are doing what I would love to do: farm for a living."

This time I did something a little different. I started telling my story to them as if I were having a safety meeting on the project with my crews. I was only supposed to speak for twenty minutes, but I added a lot about safety, trying to get their attention, and stressing that what happened to me did not have to happen to any of them. Before I left the stage, I apologized to the next speaker for using up some of her time, but she told me they needed to hear more of what I was telling them rather than what she was going to tell them.

Then she invited me to speak at one of her conferences in North Carolina.

*****

Presenting Awards to Doug Spinks (summer, 2008)

One of the things I have been truly honored to do is help present several awards to Doug Spinks. The first award came from the South Carolina Army National Guard, where Doug received the Extraordinary Achievement Medal. Lee Ann and I were asked if we would like to be there for the presentation by our friend, Dale Hall.

When we arrived, we were surprised to see our friends Tim and Terri Carraway. My sister-in-law Lori Kay joined us too. Dale met us at the door, and we had the opportunity to meet the Adjutant General of the South Carolina Army National Guard, Major General Stanhope S. Spears. While we were there the General showed us his office and shared with us what the Army National Guard is all about.

The conference room was filled with newspaper reporters, TV reporters, and more than a hundred guardsmen. All of them were there to honor Doug. When we walked in with Doug and Major General Spears, Dan Tordjman was there. He was the Channel 10 news reporter who had been covering my story from the beginning. But today was not my day. Today, it was all about Doug. Even so, Dan asked if he could put a microphone on me and I agreed.

Dale was leading the ceremony, and he began by telling his version of the story to the audience. He went into great detail about everything Doug had to do to save my life. Then Dale asked Doug and me to come up on stage. He let Doug speak and then asked me to speak.

I told Dale that I could not have told my story any better than he did. He knew it pretty well by that point. Next, Dale introduced Major General Spears, who came up on stage to present and pin the medal on Doug's uniform.

It was a huge honor for me to stand on the stage with the man who saved my life and watch him receive this high award. And it was made even better by the fact that a good friend of mine was the one to tell the story. I'll admit, it was very emotional, but I was especially proud that the South Carolina Army National Guard had recognized Doug with this honor.

Once the ceremony was over, we gathered for a reception. While we were there, I had the honor of meeting Doug's mother. I made sure to tell her right away that she had a remarkable son. Naturally, she agreed. After meeting her I wanted to talk to all the guardsmen and thank them for their service to our country, but I was only able to talk to a few of them. The various news people wanted to talk to Doug and me. I realized at that point that I should have thanked them when I was on stage, but I was too nervous.

Somehow I have to get over being nervous so I can tell people what I really think.

Not long after that, I was asked to attend a banquet for the South Carolina Firefighters Association in Myrtle Beach, South Carolina. They provided lodging accommodations for Lee Ann and me in the presidential suite. The only thing better than that was getting to spend time with Doug and many of the firefighters from across the state.

And I'm here to tell you, those guys know how to have fun.

On the day of the banquet we got to see all of the updated firefighting equipment and the new fire trucks that were on display in the convention center. We saw the new fire truck for the town of Kershaw (where Doug is a firefighter) before the people in Kershaw did. The new fire truck had been delivered straight from the factory to the convention site. It was a beautiful piece of equipment, with the most up-to-date firefighting tools.

At the awards ceremony I had the opportunity to present Doug with the Meritorious Action Award. I was again honored to be the one to present such a well-deserved honor to Doug. This award is given to a firefighter who has rendered services beyond the ordinary course of duty in an attempt to save a life, regardless of the possibility of success. That sums up perfectly what he did that September day.

*****

Story House Productions (October, 2008)

Of all the show-related experiences I have had so far, the ones with Story House Productions are some of my favorites. They produced *Swamp Brothers, Countdown to Ground Zero, Storm Riders: Chasing Fish in the North Sea,* and a number of other television series and specials for The Discovery Channel, the National Geographic Channel, and other similar venues.

One reason they are a favorite is that they included Lee Ann and Sampson Jr. They had the chance to tell their side of the story, and they are such an important part of my story before and after the accident. Another impressive thing they did was recreating the accident at the farm.

The film crew was a diverse bunch. The producer and the cameraman were from Germany, and both the audio technician and the runner were from Washington, D.C. The two from Germany flew in the day before and spent the night in Monroe, North Carolina, and the two from Washington, D.C. drove down and met with them the next morning. They all arrived at our house in North Carolina on Saturday morning, and our introductions began by sitting in my living room getting to know each other and discussing the plan. Sampson Jr. got to show off his five mounted bucks and two mallards hanging on the wall in our hunting room. The crew was impressed.

After visiting and showing the crew around the house, they were ready to get down to the business of filming. They didn't come all the way from Germany to see our home and look at hunting trophies mounted on the walls, after all. They had work to do.

Their story concept was centered around how people deal with pain. After explaining the overall theme, they briefed us on what they wanted to do. The scenes at the house were going to be shot with Lee Ann and Sampson Jr. They told me I could have the day off. So while they set up Lee Ann's interview space, I went to the store to get steaks and shrimp for dinner that night. We had invited the crew for dinner, our treat, and I was going to do the cooking. I love to grill out on our back porch, and I especially love the new grill Sampson Jr. bought for me.

My son is tight when it comes to his money. He hadn't planned on buying me or anyone else a grill. He had been to a NASCAR race a few weeks earlier and had borrowed my grill. We let him use it under one condition: if it was damaged, lost, or stolen he would have to replace it. He agreed, though neither one of us really thought anything would happen to it since we live about eight miles from the speedway. He planned to go slow both ways because of the traffic and make sure it was well secured. As I said, we all felt nothing would happen to the grill.

But things don't always work out like you plan.

On the way home he was a little less careful because the ride to the speedway went well. In fact, it went so well that he didn't tie the grill down for the return trip, and you can probably guess what happened. The grill fell off the back of his truck and was destroyed.

I was disappointed, not because he demolished it, but because that was a great grill. Even though it was at least ten years old, the lighting mechanism still worked.

Sampson Jr. looked like he was about to pass a kidney stone when we told him the grill had originally cost six hundred dollars. But he's a man of his word, and since he said he would replace it, he did.

And I got to break in my brand new grill with our guests.

After hours of filming Lee Ann describing all the things she did the day of my accident like cooking breakfast, doing dishes, going to work, they shot scenes outside a grocery store similar to the one where she was when she received the call from her mom. Then it was Sampson Jr.'s turn. They interviewed him in his room, and his interview lasted a couple of hours. When he came down the steps from his room after his interview, he looked like he was emotionally drained. No one had ever interviewed him like that before. He is a quiet kind of guy who remains pretty even keeled most of the time. But this experience opened the emotional floodgates.

The crew wanted some shots of our neighborhood, so they took their equipment and walked around filming while they still had decent light.

While they were gone, Lee Ann and I started working on dinner and setting up everything outside on the patio.

There was a full moon that night, and the weather was just perfect for grilling and eating outside. After the crew returned we stood around the grill and cooked the steaks. Sampson Jr. invited his new girlfriend, Meredith, to eat with us and meet the film crew. During dinner we asked the crew where they were from and what big names they had worked with. They all had interesting stories to tell. In fact, the cameraman had filmed Michael Jackson when he was in Germany doing a video.

The producer had been all over the world making films, and though the audio technician had worked only in the states, he had a lot of interesting stories. The runner had only worked for Story House Productions for two weeks and was still in training. After dinner they left to go to their hotel. Then for the next three days they stayed busy filming at the farm.

We met at the farm early on Sunday morning. It was a sunny day, but there was still a nip in the air. The first thing I wanted to do was to put them in what I was starting to call my "farm truck" and take them on a tour of the farm. It was the same truck I had been using the day of my accident (I eventually bought the truck from Blythe Construction to use on the farm).

It still had a few signs of blood on the interior roof that was visible if you knew where to look. So I showed them the spots. After driving them around and showing them the cabin, they were ready to get started.

The producer and the cameraman walked around the cornfield to get a better idea of how to set up the filming for that day. They had asked me weeks earlier if I still had the old picker and if it still worked. I told them we still had it and that even though some pieces were burned off it still ran, but it wouldn't pick corn. Since it worked, they had me put the corn picker in the same location where the accident had happened. Several times during the filming they asked me if it bothered me to recreate the scene. I told them that I had made peace with the picker with the help of God, and since that day it didn't bother me, but every now and then things would catch me off guard, and in those cases I would take a moment to thank God I was still alive.

The first day of filming was a lot of fun. They showed me walking through the cornfield while answering questions from the producer. We did these scenes over and over from different angles. Then they shot scenes of me picking corn with my new picker and of Sampson Jr. plowing the field that we had already picked.

The second day was cloudy, and it was hard for the cameraman to get the shots he wanted. They had to use more lights and be more creative on where they filmed.

Lee Ann had to work, but would be coming down later, and Sampson Jr. had to go to school so that second day they spent a lot of time filming me as I told my story. It was an exhausting day, partially because they asked a lot of very deep and personal questions that no one had asked before. This was harder than working on my real job, and it took a real toll on me.

The last day was the big day. I got to stand back and watch as they recreated the accident. They hired a stunt man to play me, and they recreated the fire. They also contacted Doug Spinks about having the local fire department standing by to put out the fire and keep the stunt man from getting injured. The weather forecasters called for rain off and on all day, and the farm was a mess. Because of all the plowing we had done the day before, he ground was nothing but mud.

The crew and the stunt man showed up right on time, and we all met and made a game plan. Doug and the other members of the Westville Fire Department arrived, and we were ready to set the corn picker on fire. The stunt man, who I later found out had been in one of my favorite movies (The Patriot) and a lot of other big movies, was really good. I couldn't believe I was standing there watching a stunt man playing me. He was dressed in jeans like the ones I wore, except his were covered with fire retardant. He looked just like I had looked the day of the accident except for the fact that he was wearing a long-sleeved shirt, and I had been wearing short sleeves that day. He needed the long sleeves to protect his arms from getting burned during the stunt work. Just before they were ready to shoot, they had everyone gather corn shucks to make the fire inside the picker.

While others were getting the shucks, they started shooting scenes of the stunt man driving my tractor and picking corn with my newer picker.

Then we unhooked that picker and hooked up the old one. I showed the stunt man how the accident happened so he would know what to do. Then the crew set the corn shucks on fire, and all of a sudden it looked just like the day of my accident. The only difference was that the original day had been dry, and on the day of the shooting there was a light rain falling.

The stunt man got on his knees and put his arm inside the burning picker, just like I showed him. The firefighters were ready to put the fire out if he got into trouble … and he did.

Within just a few seconds, his pants and shirt were burning. He pulled back from the fire and fell to the ground. His assistant was shouting to the fireman to put the fire out. The stunt man's pant leg was on fire, just like mine had been, and his shirt caught on fire too. After they put the fire out and the stunt man regrouped, he put on new clothes with more fire retardant. Fortunately his jeans were burned, but he wasn't. He had a talk with the producer and told her that they had cut things too close, and they needed to do some things differently. Things like not putting his arm inside the picker, and not using so much fire. She agreed and told the fireman to be ready again.

I wondered if it would be even more realistic to set the tire on fire like it was the day of the accident, but after this incident, the crew thought that might be too dangerous and didn't want anyone to get hurt. I agreed. After a few more takes the rain was really pouring so we moved to the barn to take some shots. It was probably a good thing it started raining when it did, because the stunt man was running out of pants; he had already burned up five new pairs of jeans.

We pulled the good corn picker into my barn and turned it on. The crew wanted to get a shot with the rollers moving. Shot after shot after shot they kept working on it to get the right one. One time they filled a pair of work gloves like I was wearing with fake blood and touched them to the rollers. The rollers pulled the glove in, and the fake blood sprayed everywhere. The blood even splattered the camera. They did this a number of times from different angles until they ran out of gloves.

By this time, the rain was really coming down, and all the cars were still out in the cornfield where we had set the picker on fire. I knew they were going to be stuck, so I unhooked the picker from my tractor and pulled the cars out one at a time until we got them all out.

After much conversation in German between the cameraman and the producer, they decided they had enough footage. During their conversation I didn't have a clue as to what was being said, but they looked very serious. After the stunt man and the firefighters left, the crew asked if Lee Ann and I would join them for dinner. We agreed to meet in Camden at a nice restaurant called Sam Kendall's.

The food was great, and the crew was very happy with the filming that they had done. We all sat talking until we were the last ones in the restaurant. The producer picked up the bill for everyone. I told the film crew that I couldn't believe how much work goes into making a film. Of all the filming we had done in the last four days, the show was only going to be about 30 minutes of my story and 30 minutes of a young boy in Germany who feels no pain.

As we started walking toward the door to leave the owner, Jonathan Bazinet, stopped me and asked if I was the man who had cut off his arm to save his life, and I said yes. He was so glad to meet me and shook my hand. Once outside the restaurant, we all said our goodbyes and they were off to their hotel, then back to Germany the next day. Lee Ann and I drove back to our farm for the night and returned home the next day.

All in all, it was an awesome experience with a great group of people.

*****

Rocky River Presbyterian Church (April, 2009)

I kept the promise I made to Kyle Hite back in December and started preparing my talk for his congregation at Rocky River Presbyterian Church on Easter Sunday. I figured since telling my story to millions of people on TV was scary (and nerve-wracking), surely telling my story to the 400 or so members of his church would be a piece of cake.

Yes, that's what I thought.

Then I thought about it some more and realized I had never stood up in church to say anything before. The more I thought about it, the more I realized this was going to be my biggest challenge so far. Speaking on camera was not so bad because all you have to do is focus on the person asking you the question. Plus, by now you would think I would be getting pretty good at sharing my story, but it is still difficult for me to talk about myself.

To some, my story is about someone who made a bad decision and now has to live with the consequences. To others, it is a story of keeping hope alive, and some people find comfort and inspiration in that. I have come to realize through much prayer that sharing my experience with others is God's purpose for me. I am here to help others who have no hope and to share story of God's grace.

Two weeks before the Sunday on which I was to speak, I met with Kyle. We sat outside the church one evening and talked about my story and why he wanted me to share it with the congregation. He said people needed to hear that there is a living God who works in the lives of people.

When I told him how nervous I was, he suggested that I stand behind the pulpit with no one in the church and practice my story. He said standing behind the pulpit with people sitting in the pews gives you the feeling of sharing something very powerful.

Lee Ann and I worked for at least two weeks on how I was going to present my story on Easter. She is so good to me and is so smart. I respect her ideas when it comes to ways of telling my story to others. She is good at knowing what parts are appropriate for different kinds of audiences. For example, you probably don't want to spend a lot of time talking to the ladies at the garden club about how far the blood was spurting from the stump of your freshly severed arm.

I wasn't the best student in school. My focus wasn't English and public speaking, so when it was time to speak in class, I would work harder on getting out of speaking than I did on the speech. I would even skip class or give the teacher some kind of excuse just so I wouldn't have to stand up in front of class and read or present something. Somehow I managed to get out of speaking all through school, and now I truly regret it. Without Lee Ann's help, I would never have the nerve to do what I was going to do, and I knew deep down that as much as I hated speaking in front of people, God wanted me to share my story. So telling it on Easter Sunday was going to be an honor for me. But it was also going to be a little scary.

I thought being on the *Today Show* was a nerve-wracking experience. Even though there were supposed to be twenty million people watching, I couldn't see them. But the thought of standing in a pulpit looking out over the congregation in a packed church on Easter Sunday and telling my story to every person in there made me weak and sick to my stomach. But with Lee Ann's help, we worked on how to present the story in a manner that would be suitable for the congregation. I started practicing in the church as Kyle suggested, and he was right. By standing there and practicing with just Lee Ann in the church, I saw what he had been talking about. The way the church is designed, standing in the pulpit allows the preacher to look out over the congregation and feel like he is speaking to every person individually. And something about being in that particular place does give you a feeling that what you are saying is special.

I understood why Kyle wanted me to tell my story, but the thing I didn't understand was why he wanted me to do it on Easter. That and Christmas are the two biggest times of the year for most churches. So I asked him why he wanted me to speak on Easter instead of a different Sunday.

He said he wanted a full house so as many people as possible could hear the story, and there would certainly be a full house that day. He said he felt that the congregation needed to hear my story of real grace and that this message would ring out hope through our risen Savior and Lord, Jesus Christ.

Easter Sunday arrived, and I realized that I knew many of the people who were there that day. Lee Ann, Sampson Jr., and I arrived at the church with my brother Steve, his wife, Delia, their son, Colt, and Delia's mother, Nancy, who was visiting them from Kentucky. When we walked into the church, there in the back middle pews were my in-laws, Keith and Helen. They surprised us by coming up from their home in Camden, South Carolina. When Kyle came over I introduced everyone to him, and he welcomed them all. Kyle took a few minutes to tell me what was going to happen and said he would introduce me to the church. Then, it was all up to me. Oh man, what had I gotten myself into? My hands were sweating, and my legs were shaking.

When Kyle introduced me, the congregation applauded and I was touched by their welcome. I walked up the steps and stood behind the pulpit looking out over a room filled with people of all ages.

It looked a lot different from when all the pews were empty.

I said a quick, silent prayer and asked God to help me not be so nervous, and to let my story help someone there today who may have challenges in his or her own life.

I started out by thanking Kyle and the congregation for giving me the opportunity to share my story with the church. After a shaky start, I finally calmed down and was able to tell my story.

At the end of the service, I stood by the front doors with Kyle so that I could greet the people coming out and have the opportunity to shake everyone's hand. So many people told me how much I inspired them and how they felt blessed to hear the whole story. Many of them had only heard bits and pieces of what had actually happened, but never heard the whole story. The news media in North Carolina never picked up my story the way the media in South Carolina had.

Following all the goodbyes and best wishes, we went home and had lunch. I was emotionally drained, and all I wanted to do was get out and go for a drive somewhere. Lee Ann and I took off for a random drive and ended up at Baden Lake. We looked at houses and checked out available property. We have always talked about owning a home on a lake. It was relaxing to dream about the future and discuss which home we would pick if we were making a purchase right then.

*****

The Easter holiday was over, and it was time to get back to work. Once again I had to shift gears and focus on getting the current highway project finished. It was very hard for me to stay focused with so many people still wanting to hear my story. I really had to dig deep within myself and pray a lot to keep this from going to my head.

I believe that having the opportunity to tell and retell my story was part of my healing process. I often wondered about people who had been in situations similar to mine; people who had suffered pain and loss, but didn't have the audiences and other people who wanted to hear about what had happened to them, people who had no kind of outside support. I was free to talk about my accident and not hold anything back. Most people are not so fortunate. I wondered how they vented. I wondered how they felt when they weren't able to use their experience to encourage and help someone else.

I still give thanks to God for this opportunity, and I continue to pray and listen for His guidance. In fact, that's why I am writing my story. Hundreds of people have said, "Sampson, you need to share this with other people and show them that the power of God is real. You need to write a book."

I fought the idea of writing a book about my experience for a long time, mostly because I wanted to be sure this was coming from God, and not just my own ego. But the idea kept coming back, and I know now that this is what God had in mind.

*****

The World of Politics (September, 2009)

My sister-in-law, Sheri Few, asked me to tell my story at a political event that was to be held on the courthouse steps in Camden, South Carolina. The event just happened to be held on the second anniversary of my accident. And since a lot of people had heard about me and had seen me on TV, she hoped this would help in bringing more people out to the event. Many people, including me, don't take the time to attend these types of political events. But after having been to this event and hearing the various people speak, I realized it was a lot different than what I thought it would be, in a positive way.

I was the keynote speaker for the event, and to my surprise, they had also asked Doug Spinks to speak. He was going to talk about firefighters. With this being September 11th, it was appropriate to have a firefighter who was also a serviceman speak at this event. And who better to do it than Doug? My part was to tell my story and to introduce my sister-in-law to the crowd. She was going to announce that she was seeking the Republican nomination for the State House, in South Carolina. This would be her second attempt for this seat. She almost won the previous election, and here she was mounting another campaign. She is a fighter like me.

Lee Ann and I had fine-tuned my story so that it would fit the theme of not giving up. Sheri's point that day was that we should not give up on the current political situation, but rather, stand up for our political views and passions.

As I told my story, I could see many people with tears in their eyes, including Sheri. She had never heard the whole story with all the details. While I was talking, one lady fainted. I was shocked and didn't know what I was supposed to do. I couldn't help wondering if it was because of the graphic details I was including in my story.

Since I wasn't sure what to do, I just kept talking. My mother-in-law was there, and she helped the lady who passed out, since she was the first person to get to her. A few minutes later, she and some other coworkers had her up and drinking water.

Later I found out she was dehydrated, so she didn't actually pass out because of what I was saying.

*****

Bethel Worship Center (August, 2010)

I was asked to be a special guest speaker at a Vacation Bible School Boot Camp for Women at the Bethel Worship Center in Camden, South Carolina.

The nightly lessons were to be taught by Denise Hildreth Jones, the author of the *Savannah From Savannah* series and *Flies on the Butter*. So when I was asked to speak, I didn't think about it for a second. I just agreed to do it. Later, when I found out there were going to be over 400 women at the camp, I almost fainted.

Once again I wondered what I had gotten myself into.

One Saturday night after I agreed to speak, Lee Ann and I were at Leos in Lugoff for supper. While we were there, I saw a flyer advertising the *Boot Camp: The Whole Woman Revolution*. And there on the flyer was a picture of me along with the other guest speakers: Mary Kay Beard (founder of Angel Tree), Hannah Horne (program MC and morning news anchor at WIS TV in Columbia), and Denise Hildreth Jones. I was shocked. I still couldn't believe they wanted *me*, just an ordinary guy, to speak at this event. Between the numbers of women I'd be speaking to and the well-known guests I'd be speaking with, I'm not ashamed to admit that I was feeling a little intimidated.

But I knew I would keep my word, so I did a lot of praying before the event. Lee Ann helped me prepare my story so it would fit with their theme, and she also helped me take out some of the gruesome details.

On the day I was to share my story, we drove down to Camden, and I talked almost nonstop about how nervous I was just thinking about standing up and speaking in front of all those women. Lee Ann kept telling me to pray about it. She said to ask God to turn this self-directed anxiety around and make it into a positive energy that would somehow help someone that night.

When we arrived we were taken into a side room to meet with the other speakers and go over the night's schedule with Denise and Hannah. They were so relaxed. And they all said they were excited about the chance to hear my story. They had all heard bits and pieces, but none of them had heard the full story.

After a while a woman came in and said we had five minutes to go, and then she put a microphone on Denise, and then put one on me. We were walking out of the room when Lee Ann asked if we could join in prayer before we went. Everyone gathered around and held hands as she led us in prayer. My prayer was that God would ease my nerves and not let me faint in front of all these women. While she prayed, I also prayed and asked God to let my story inspire at least one person, or help one person to know there is a loving God who is full of grace no matter what their situation may be.

We walked in, and the auditorium was packed.

Standing room only.

The first person I saw was Pete Rabon, Terri Carraway's father. Pete came because he wanted to hear my story firsthand. As we made our way to the front, I saw Karen Baker, the nurse who stopped to help me. I gave her a big hug and thanked her for coming. While I was sharing my story, I made a point to recognize Karen and publicly thanked her for stopping to help me. The crowd of women broke out in applause to honor her Good Samaritan efforts. My mother-in-law, Helen, and my sister-in-law,

Sheri, were seated right behind where we were going to be seated. In fact, Sheri had been asked to introduce me. She did a great job. Helen probably sensed I was nervous because she reached up to give me a pat on the back and told me I would do great.

I felt much calmer knowing that there were people in the audience that I knew. And of course my number one fan, Lee Ann, was right there beside me.

The next thing I knew, the church band got on the stage and the place started rocking. This was my first experience with a contemporary church atmosphere, but it didn't take long for me to feel the power of the Holy Spirit. I forgot all about being nervous and just started worshiping through the band's music. And I wasn't the only one. By this time the whole crowd was fired up.

As the band finished up its song, Hannah got up to welcome everyone and then introduced Sheri, who led us in prayer. Then Sheri introduced me. I walked up to the stage, gave Sheri a big hug, and thanked her for the introduction. I told the audience that, after hearing the introduction, I was convinced she knew more about me than I did.

I began by telling the ladies that the guys would be so jealous if they knew how much fun their wives and girlfriends were having. After a laugh, I shared my story with a sense of calm that I had never experienced before. I felt I was truly being led by the Holy Spirit. And when I finished, I was humbled by the standing ovation gifted to me by these special women. God was truly with me that night because I would have never in a million years been able to pull that off without Him. In fact, between the band and the receptive crowd, this has been my favorite speaking engagement so far.

On the way home I told Lee Ann how much fun it had been. What a change from the drive down. But it also reminded me of something very important.

God has a plan for each of us. But even so, we still have a choice. We can abide by His plan, or we can run from it. For me, no matter how hard something seems, if I pray about it and ask for God's help, He is always there for me.

And He'll be there for you too.

*****

The BBC's Pleasure and Pain with Michael Mosley (January, 2011)

One of my favorite TV show interviews to date was for a program called *Pleasure and Pain with Michael Mosley* that was aired on the BBC in England. This show examines why pleasure and pain are essential for human survival by combining science and real life experiences. Two producers (Esther and Debbie) and a cameraman came all the way from England to my farm to do the interview.

About halfway through my story (the gory part), Esther started to faint. Fortunately we caught her before she hit the ground and gave her a bottle of water. After a few minutes she said she was okay and ready to get back to work, saying it must have been the heat. We all nodded and didn't make too much of it, but deep down we all knew it was really the part about the blood shooting out about three feet from the stump of my arm that got to her.

Even so, the interview went great and only took about four hours to complete. The producers had done their homework and already knew a lot of the story when they arrived, so they knew what questions they wanted to ask well ahead of time. To their credit, when it came to the parts of my story about God, they didn't cut a single one. A couple months later they sent us a DVD of the show, and I was impressed at how they had put it all together. Again, they didn't cut out any of my praise and glory to God.

But they did cut out the part where Esther almost fainted.

Not long after that, I was amazed at how fast this show spread across YouTube and Facebook. Then again, God has used stranger methods to get His message across to people. So once again I prayed that my story might somehow help someone who was in need.

CHAPTER 19

The Last Word

Even though I didn't attend church at the time all of this happened, I did believe in God and I had what I thought was a strong faith. And when I called out for God's help, He helped me. That's pretty simplistic, but some truths are that simple.

That being said, some people may look at my story and think that things happening the way they did was pure coincidence, but I know better. I know that no matter who or what you are, God will never forget about you or leave you.

Every day I remember that it is God who makes it possible for me to be here. It is God who has given me the strength to wake up every morning with a thankful heart and the ability to go about every task with a positive "can do'" attitude. When I start feeling a little down or get frustrated, I pray about what is bothering me and always ask for God's guidance. I know He is here for me.

Before my accident, I would never have gotten up in front of anyone and told them how I felt about God. My religious beliefs and my relationship with God were private. Now I find myself getting up in front of hundreds of people to tell them about our loving God, His gift of grace, and how He is part of my daily life. Before the accident no one at work knew anything about my religious beliefs, and I didn't know anything about theirs. I was just a tough guy with no apparent feelings. But things change.

Now I am more open about my faith. On the one hand, I wish I had always been that way, but on the other hand, maybe I'm able to appreciate this new life I've found more because of what Lee Ann and I have been through to get here.

So now that I've laid everything out there in the open, what do I hope you'll take from this book?

I hope that you will come to know that no matter where you are in your relationship with God, whether you have one or not, He is there for you. I hope that you'll remember in times of loss, depression, and hardship to never give up, no matter how tough things get. God is always there for you.

And there's one final thing. Remember in the beginning when I said love saved my life? Well, that's doubly true. God saved me out there on the farm. But long before that, He gave me another great gift in my wife, Lee Ann, and her love for me.

*****

Well, that's about it. As I've said before, I'm a simple man. I never would have dreamed something like this would happen to me. And I certainly never thought God would use me to reach out to others.

But that's what happened, and that's what I'm doing.

I hope my story will inspire you to never give up. To think about life a little differently. To remember how precious life is. And above all I hope you'll know that through God you can find the strength to move on after suffering tragedy and loss because life will go back to normal, or a new version of normal. And yes, normal may change, but that's not necessarily a bad thing. Through this ordeal, I have learned things about myself, about my family, and about friends that I will cherish the rest of my life. And through all of this I now recognize my purpose, to share the Good News and God's wonderful grace.

"But my life is worth nothing to me unless I use it for finishing
the work assigned me by the Lord Jesus – the work of telling others the
Good News about the wonderful grace of God."
Acts 20:24